HEAVENLY SONG

HEAVENLY SONG

Stories of Church of God Song Writers and Their Songs

KATHLEEN D. BUEHLER

Warner Press, Inc.
Anderson, Indiana

Copyright © 1993 by Warner Press, Inc.
ISBN #0-87162-647-0   Stock #D4301
All rights reserved
Printed in the United States of America
Warner Press, Inc

Arlo F. Newell, Editor in Chief
Dan Harman, Book Editor
Cover by Larry Lawson

Contents

Preface

One need not look far into this volume to realize that it is not an exhaustive hymnal anthology. Neither does it list all the song writers or songs of our movement's tradition.

I have, with this volume, tried to give information on most of our early song writers and composers, as well as some of the songs attributed to them. Much of the material will be recognized as having appeared at some time from 1989 to 1991 in the "Songs of Faith" column of *Vital Christianity*. This material has been edited as new data has surfaced and has been compiled into one resource.

The songs chosen for this volume are all part of the newest Church of God hymnal *Worship the Lord* (1990). All of the songs date back fifty years or more. Many of the ones included are those whose creation was tied to particular circumstances—but not all. As noted by C. W. Naylor, "Most of the songs that I have written have nothing of interest connected with their origin. Often just the subject comes into mind and with it a sort of inspiration to write" (*Gospel Trumpet*, August 24, 1922, 9). Others of our movement's early poets and composers likely would have agreed. Some of the song poems and tunes were written of necessity as the editors compiled a new songbook and found they needed a song on a particular theme.

Two alphabetical indexes have been added to aid the reader in finding a particular song writer or song.

Acknowledgments

Without the records of Church of God historians and biographers and the writings of the authors and composers themselves in the *Gospel Trumpet* and elsewhere, this book could not exist. I am grateful for the foresight of these persons.

My thanks also goes to the families of some of these writers and composers, who helped clarify, correct, or add to information already on hand. I am grateful to God for the rich heritage in song and faith that we in the Church of God possess and I give thanks for the opportunity to research some of that history and heritage.

D. S. Warner and his "company"
(Left to right) Barney E. Warren, D. S. Warner,
Nancy Kigar, Sarah Smith, Frankie Miller

Introduction: The Gospel in Song

Almost from the beginning, the Church of God reformation sang its message of truth. Of the two men publishing the *Gospel Trumpet* in the early days, D. S. Warner was a poet and J. C. Fisher could write both words and music.

As early as 1885, Fisher had compiled and published a songbook (*Songs of Victory*) that was printed in Grand Junction, Michigan. The songbook, according to the preface, was "specially adapted to the holiness work, in camp meetings, revivals, and all the assemblies of the saints of the Most High God." Three years later, the Gospel Trumpet Company published its first songbook *Anthems from the Throne* with Warner and Barney E. Warren as the main contributors.

A. L. Byers, in his biographical book on Warner, devoted a whole chapter to "The Ministry of Song." He wrote, "One of the prominent features of the reformation was the sweet, heavenly singing of the saints."[1]

Warner formed a company of singers to travel with him on his evangelistic trips. "Wherever Brother Warner's company went," Byers wrote, "the people were attracted by the singing. They were not what the world would call 'trained singers'; they were not even adept at reading music. But God blessed the singing, so that the songs, sung in the element of the Spirit, were simply heavenly."[2]

Stories have remained about the effects of the singing. One is told of a meeting held in Walkerton, Indiana, at the same time a theatrical troupe was there. People had come to hear D. S. Warner and his company, leaving few to attend the theatrical concert. The troupe came to the meeting, stood just outside, and played instrumental music to attract the crowd to them. Warner was trying to preach. He stopped and called for a song. The company began singing, and the people stayed with Warner.[3]

In Spring 1894 an evangelistic trip was begun on the Floating Bethel—a traveling church on a barge—down the Ohio River. H. M. Riggle and his wife joined the gospel

The Floating Bethel

workers on that trip. According to his account, singing was an important part of their program.

"We stopped at about all towns and cities on both sides of the Ohio," wrote Riggle. "As soon as we safely anchored, we would gather on the [flat] roof of the boat and sing. Through curiosity, great crowds assembled. This gave us a fine opportunity to announce our meetings and reach a host of people. Many congregations were thus raised up in these river towns."[4]

The early songwriters put their theology into their songs, and Church of God people sang as well as preached the truth. They seemed to realize the importance of music to the cause of spreading the gospel. "Music is heavenly and divine," reads the preface of one of the early songbooks. "There is great power in spiritual song. The gospel in song often moves and melts hearts that preaching cannot touch."[5]

1

Daniel S. Warner:
The Poet Preacher

Daniel Sidney was born in 1842 to David and Leah Warner, the fifth child in the family. His father was a tavern keeper in Ohio, but later the family moved to a farm. "The Warren family," wrote A. L. Byers, "though clever, straightforward, and strictly honest, were but a simple rural folk and not inclined to religion."[1] Daniel, however, was, according to C. E. Brown, "by nature a deeply religious man."[2]

Warner was converted in February 1865 in a country schoolhouse revival meeting. He went that same year to Oberlin College for further education. When he felt God calling him to the ministry, he left college to prepare himself through Bible study and prayer and whatever else he felt ministerial preparation required.

Warner affiliated himself with the General Eldership of the Churches of God in North America, founded by John Winebrenner, and became a minister with that group. He became quite a popular preacher. "His deep sincerity and utter unselfishness, growing constantly with the inner fire of the Spirit, made him a preacher much sought after wherever he was known."[3]

He came to believe in and preach sanctification and holiness, which got him in trouble with the Winebrennarian group. Meanwhile he became coeditor of a publication called the *Herald of Gospel Freedom*.

In 1881 he officially broke away from the General

D. S. Warner

Eldership and also became the sole editor of the paper that by this time had joined with another under the name *Gospel Trumpet*. Through this paper he began to publish his beliefs of sanctification and holiness. He was not alone. A group of persons of like mind drew around him in the preaching of the Word and in the publishing work. The Church of God reformation movement was born.

Warner formed an evangelistic team of singers and traveled

4

with them for five years, holding meetings in many areas of the United States and in Canada.

Though plagued with ill health and a frail physical condition, Warner kept a fast pace in the gospel work. He traveled from place to place for evangelistic meetings, many times dealing with uncomfortable traveling conditions and sleeping accommodations and with opposition to his message.

Warner knew suffering and loss in his personal life. He and his friend and coeditor J. D. Fisher parted company over a moral issue in Fisher's life. Warner lost his first wife, Tamzen, in death, along with four infant children. His second wife, Sarah, left him and their young son, Sidney, renouncing the reformation message she had once claimed. Warner's efforts at reconciliation proved fruitless.

After Sarah's death, Warner married Frances Miller, who had been a member of his evangelistic team.

Warner visited and prayed for the sick and kept up a great deal of correspondence. He wrote articles for and edited the *Gospel Trumpet,* and he still found time to write poetry for songs and to keep up a personal diary.

Warner was a poet at heart, and in 1890 he gathered a number of his poems in a book called *Poems of Grace and Truth.* It was the first major clothbound book (343 pages in size) made at the Gospel Trumpet office.

Warner also wrote song poems. A. L. Byers said that Warner had a gift for song writing, but that "the development of this came, however, only with his entrance upon the special work of the reformation. . . . Considering the little time he had to devote to the study of those principles [of hymn writing], it is marvelous that he produced so many useful, and we may say excellent, hymns during the few short years of his intensive ministerial labor."[4]

At first he adapted hymns—took existing hymn tunes and changed around the words or wrote entirely new words. He was not a writer of tunes. Later he teamed up with tune writers; B. E. Warren wrote the music for many of Warner's song poems. Two songbooks, *Anthems from the Throne* (1888) and *Echoes from Glory* (1893), carry as the bulk of songs those written cooperatively by Warner and Warren. Warner died on December 12, 1895, from a sickness that had developed into pneumonia. But Warner had made a difference with his life. In writing of his story, Byers wrote that he hoped readers would see in Warner "an example of true consecration, devotion, courage, diligence, humility, faith, patience, kindness, self-denial, and the Christian graces generally, that is worthy of being followed."[5]

The Bond of Perfectness

Christian fellowship, or the communion of saints, was a subject often preached and sung by D. S. Warner and other early pioneers.

Barney Warren told of one such time during a meeting at Yellow Lake, Indiana, in the early 1890s.[6] D. S. Warner and B. E. Warren were in attendance, as well as other early leaders. During the service several speakers talked of Christian fellowship, of the love that binds Christians together. One speaker said, "Christian fellowship means a lot of fellows in one ship."

After a while an elderly pioneer, Brother Hartung, stood and, in broken English, said, "Fellowship! Why brethren, fellowship means to stick together. Then, if we don't have this bond of fellowship, we do not stick together!"

Meanwhile, Warner was composing words that would become the first verse and chorus of the song "The Bond of Perfectness." After the service, he handed Warren the piece of paper on which he had written the words. Warren went right to the organ and began to play in the key of E flat. The song was finished in short order. It was first published in 1893 in *Echoes from Glory.*

6

I Know My Name Is There

Following is the account of how this song came into being, as expressed by B. E. Warren.[7]

> During an evangelistic campaign, D. S. Warner suggested that we have a short testimony service just before he began preaching. Many testified. Among those who gave their experiences were two women who spoke doubtfully as to a positive knowledge of their salvation.
>
> One woman said, "I think I am a Christian."
>
> Another one said, "I believe that I profess to be a Christian."
>
> Brother Warner, desiring to convince the woman of the necessity of knowing that her sins were forgiven, said to her, "Sister, are you married?"
>
> She answered that she was.
>
> "Do you have a home?" he asked.
>
> "Yes, I have," was her reply.
>
> "Then, if you have a home," Brother Warner continued, "how do you know that it is yours?"
>
> Emphatically she answered, "We paid for it, and we have a clear title to it."
>
> This was Brother Warner's opportunity to preach her a short sermon. "You can know just as positively that you are saved," he said. "The Bible says, 'To give knowledge of salvation unto his people by the remission of their sins' (Luke 1:77), and, 'The Spirit itself beareth witness with our spirit, that we are the children of God.' "
>
> The woman seemed puzzled.
>
> Brother Warner continued, "If we do not have a positive knowledge of salvation, we are allowing Satan to deceive us."
>
> After a short time the woman seemed to see new light and to visualize her privilege as a Christian through the promise of grace in Christ.

Another woman arose, and during her testimony said, "I know my name is there in the Book of Life."

This service gave thought and inspiration to the writing of the words of "I Know My Name Is There."

His Yoke Is Easy

The text for a sermon D. S. Warner preached in 1892 was Matthew 11:29-30: "Take my yoke upon you, and learn of me. . . . For my yoke is easy, and my burden is light." B. E. Warren told how during this service, a young woman was converted. When she rose from the altar, she said, "His yoke is easy!"

"In a day or two the song poem was given to me," wrote Warren, "by the author, D. S. Warner. At an opportune time, I tried for a suitable melody, and with little effort the words were set to the music which is now being used. When I called Brother Warner to help me sing it, he said, 'This song will sing its way into the hearts of the people.' "[8]

The song appeared that next year in *Echoes from Glory.*

My Soul Is Satisfied

"My Soul Is Satisfied" is just one of many that the team of D. S. Warner and B. E. Warren brought into being. The song made its first published appearance in the songbook *Echoes from Glory.* The year was 1893.

About the writing of the song, Warren wrote that it came from an occasion when they were talking and listening to a group of young people. These young people had tried one way and another, searching for a thrilling life. They had not found anything truly satisfying. Warren wrote:

One young man had spent all that was left to him when his father died. He had traveled over the world in luxurious and riotous living until his inheritance was

The Bond of Perfectness

"And over all these virtues put on love, which binds them all together in perfect unity."—Colossians 3:14

Daniel S. Warner

8.7.8.7. wR.
PERFECTNESS
Barney E. Warren

1 How sweet this bond of per - fect-ness, The won-drous love of Je - sus!
2 O praise the Lord for love di - vine That binds us all to - geth- er!
3 "God o - ver all and in us all," Thru sis - ter and thru bro-ther,
4 O mys - ter - y of heav-en's peace! O bond of heav - en's un-ion!

1 A pure fore-taste of heav - en's bliss, O fel - low-ship so pre - cious!
2 A thou-sand cords our hearts en - twine For - ev - er and for - ev - er.
3 No pow'r of earth or hell, with - al, Can rend us from each oth - er.
4 Our souls in fel - low - ship em-brace, And live in sweet com-mun - ion.

Be - lov - ed, how this per - fect love U - nites us all in Je - sus! One

heart, and soul, and mind: we prove The un - ion heav - en gave us.

9

spent. When he returned home he said to some of his friends, "What a fool I have been to think that I could buy satisfaction with money and thus drown the ranklings of a guilty conscience, by rushing from one thrilling thing to another!"

Others of this group told of similar experiences. Brother Warner seemed to be in profound meditation regarding these people. Presently he looked up, and with an expression of satisfaction on his face, said, "My soul is satisfied!"

After a short time he submitted to me the [fourth] verse and chorus. My soul was already stirred with the fullness of joy. From an inner sense of satisfaction and a touch of inspiration I set the words to the simple music which is still singing the grand experience of a satisfied soul.[9]

Who Will Suffer with the Savior?

"Who Will Suffer with the Savior?" was written by D. S. Warner while he and his company of singers were on a tour in the southern United States. In a community near Meridian, Mississippi, the company found resistance to their message. Some persons in the community formed a mob and attacked the meeting place during a service, throwing bricks and clubs through windows. D. S. Warner received a cut on his face.

In writing to *Trumpet* readers about the experience, Warner said, "The glory of God was greatly upon us through all the evening, and with the cowardly onslaught, the heavenly tides so wondrously swelled in our soul that we had to leap for joy in the midst of the uproar. O the mighty river of peace and joy!"[10]

Soon after this experience, Warner wrote the words of the song, which was first titled "Who Will Suffer with Jesus?" Ludolph Schroeder wrote the tune, and B. E. Warren added harmony. The song appeared in the 1893 *Echoes from Glory.*

2

Joseph C. Fisher:
Breaking New Ground

While D. S. Warner was struggling in Indiana with his stand on denominationalism, another group of people in Michigan was struggling with it, too. Led by Joseph C. Fisher, these persons had heard Warner preach and had accepted the doctrine of sanctification. In 1881, shortly after Warner left the Winebrennarian church group, Fisher and about eighteen other persons in the Michigan group also left that denomination to become part of the Church of God reformation movement.

That fall, Fisher became involved in the publishing of the *Gospel Trumpet*, at first from a distance monetarily and as a corresponding editor.

J. C. Fisher was a prominent evangelist in those beginning days of the Church of God movement. As did Warner, Fisher held evangelistic meetings. He was influential in the states of Michigan, Ohio, Iowa, Kansas, Pennsylvania, and Arkansas. Often from these meetings, churches sprang up and new leaders were brought into the movement.

In his biography of D. S. Warner and the beginnings of the reformation movement, A. L. Byers spoke of Fisher's efforts as an evangelist. He said, "He was a very effectual preacher. It was through his efforts that the original company was raised up at Carson City, Mich. . . . Also it was through his instrumentality that the work was started in southwestern Michigan and in some other parts of the country."[1]

When the Gospel Trumpet office moved to Williamston,

Michigan, in 1884, Fisher and his wife, Allie, joined Warner in the work. He took a more active role in the business end of the publishing work as well as becoming a coeditor with Warner. He and Warner began signing their various editorials and articles with "Joseph" and "Daniel."

Besides holding meetings, writing articles, and seeing to the publishing business, Fisher found some time to compose music and write song poems. In 1885 he put a group of songs contributed mainly by Warner, H. R. Jeffrey, and himself together in a book called *Songs of Victory.* "I'm Redeemed," for which Fisher wrote both words and music, is still included in our hymnals.

Then in 1887 a crisis occurred in Fisher's life and eventually in the Gospel Trumpet Company. Fisher became involved in conduct that went contrary to the teachings of the movement.

Andrew Byers explained it this way: "A sad defection from the ranks of those who had been active in the reformation work was that of J. C. Fisher. . . . Through a lack of his consecration, sad to say, he became unfaithful in his marriage relation and found affinity with another. After being patiently and faithfully counseled by Brother Warner and others, and after it became evident that he was rejecting all admonition, and in fact had married another woman, he had to be renounced and cut off from the fellowship of the saints."[2]

D. S. Warner felt he could not continue to publish with Fisher. Fisher's interests in the publishing house were bought for one thousand dollars.

In his book on the Church of God publishing house, Harold L. Phillips observed this about the crisis: "It was a sad time for Warner because Joseph had been a staunch supporter and friend, but efforts to rescue him failed at least for the time."[3]

Whether Fisher repented and came back into fellowship, I do not know, but he never came back to prominence. The good he, through the Lord's guidance, had done in those six

J. C. Fisher

years with the movement, however, lived on in the songs he penned, the leaders he had counseled, and the churches that sprang up under his preaching.

I Ought to Love My Savior

"But God demonstrates his own love for us in this: While we were still sinners, Christ died for us."—Romans 5:8

7.6.7.6.D.

Daniel S. Warner

FISHER
Joseph C. Fisher

1. I ought to love my Sav - ior; He loved me long a - go,
2. I ought to love my Sav - ior; He bore my sin and shame;
3. I ought to love my Sav - ior; He par-doned all my sin,
4. O Christ, I can but love Thee: What heart could e'er with - hold

1. Looked on my soul with fa - vor, When deep in guilt and woe:
2. From glo - ry to the man - ger On wings of love He came:
3. Then sanc - ti - fied my na - ture, And keeps me pure with - in:
4. A love that cost so dear - ly The of - f'ring of Thy soul?

1. And though my sin had grieved Him, His Fa - ther's law had crossed,
2. He trod this earth in sor - row, En - dured the pains of hell,
3. He fills me with His glo - ry, And bears my soul a - bove;
4. O King of love im - mor - tal, Reign in my heart a - lone,

1. Love drew Him down from heav - en To seek and save the lost,
2. That I should not be ban - ished, But in His glo - ry dwell,
3. This world, O won - drous sto - ry! 'Tis love, re-deem - ing love,
4. And flood this earth - en tem - ple With glo - ry from Thy throne,

14

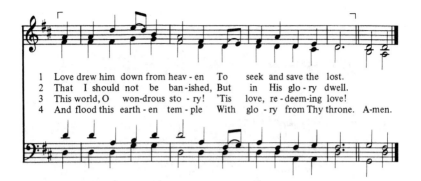

1 Love drew him down from heav-en   To   seek and save the lost.
2 That I should not be ban-ished, But   in   His glo-ry dwell.
3 This world, O won-drous sto-ry!   'Tis   love, re-deem-ing love!
4 And flood this earth-en tem-ple   With   glo-ry from Thy throne. A-men.

I Ought to Love My Savior

"I Ought to Love My Savior" came into being in the beginning years of the Church of God reformation movement. It was a collaboration between D. S. Warner and J. C. Fisher, then coeditors of the *Gospel Trumpet*. Andrew Byers referred to the song some thirty-five years later as a "hymn that breathes a deep spirit of devotion."[4]

The song appeared in the 1885 songbook *Songs of Victory*. This small songbook published by Fisher, was the first connected with the movement. This venture of publishing songbooks, according to late Church of God historian John W. V. Smith, "would prove to be one of the most important factors in propagating the movement for many decades."[5] Many of these early songs of the Church of God were not only singable, but they "lyricized the theology and the spirit of the movement."[6]

J. C. Fisher compiled this collection of ninety-four songs to which he and Warner were major contributors. Perhaps his hope for these songs is summed up in these words from the forward to *Songs of Victory*: "We fervently pray that these inspired melodies and hymns may stir and awaken the hearts of the impenitent, and that thousands of souls may be washed in the blood, and added to the Lord through their instrumentality."

Barney E. Warren and family

3

Barney E. Warren:
The Versatile, Prolific Composer

When Barney E. Warren was born in February 1867, the third of ten children, he inherited a musical family. Both his parents, Thomas G. and Anna Maria, sang, and as the children grew up, the family discovered they had a "double quartet."[1] They enjoyed singing the songs of Stephen Foster, "but best of all they loved to sing the hymns of the church."[2]

During Warren's preschool years, the family lived on a farm near Buffalo, New York. When Barney was five, they moved to Van Buren, Michigan.

In 1884 Warren was converted in a revival in a log house near Bangor, Michigan. Two years later, he had joined D. S. Warner and his evangelistic company as the bass singer.

For five years Warren traveled with Warner. The evangelistic company held meetings mostly in the midwest United States, though they did hold some meetings in other states as well. Besides Warner and Warren, that first group included Mother Sarah Smith, Nancy M. Kigar (who later married Warren), and Frances Miller (who later married Warner).

Warren had studied music composition, technique, harmony, and hymnology and had attacked his studies with eagerness and energy. "So eager was he for advancement and so filled with delight to find his growing powers released in beauty and harmony that he sometimes forgot to sleep,"[3] wrote Axchie Bolitho in her biography of Warren.

During his travels with the Warner company, Warren put these skills to use. He set much of Warner's poetry to music. A common occurrence was for Warner to scribble out words to a verse of song on a piece of paper and hand the paper to Warren, who would go to work and set it to music in a short time.

Some seven thousand gospel songs are attributed to Warren's composition. But Warren could also write lyrics. Late Church of God historian John W. V. Smith wrote, "When the second songbook, *Anthems from the Throne*, was published in 1888, Warren was not only coeditor with Warner, but he also wrote the music of seventy-eight of the ninety songs included in the book. He had poetic skills, too, for he wrote the lyrics for twenty-three of these songs."[4]

W. Dale Oldham called Warren a "versatile composer, writing not only songs of praise, but songs which provided instruction and challenge. . . . He did not ride a hobby but wrote hymns on many themes. And his own God-given talents, his ear for melody, his vivid imagination, and his emotional drive gave him the ability to make all of his songs singable."[5]

Warren was a preacher as well as a musician. After his travels with Warner ended, he continued to hold evangelistic meetings. He also held pastorates in Ohio, Florida, Maryland, and West Virginia.

Though he was not a permanent worker at the Gospel Trumpet Company, Warren worked on the production of the songbooks and hymnals for the Church of God from 1888 until the 1940s. He made "a major contribution to the music of the Church of God for more than half a century."[6] Today, more than forty years after his death in April 1951, that contribution remains an influence in the singing of the Church of God.

Beautiful

This song was born quickly out of a time of meditation. Warren explained:

One lovely spring morning in the year of 1896, I was meditating on the beauties of nature all around me. I was filled with admiration as I paused in wonderment, beholding the works of God in nature. My thoughts began to rise higher and higher to the realms of bliss in the heavenly world. I began to think in comparative terms: if the great God so loved man that he made all of the beautiful things of earth for his comfort and well-being just for time's short duration, how much more beautiful would he make those eternal things in the "place which he has gone to prepare for those who love him."

Two thoughts were in my mind—thoughts of earthly and heavenly things. I immediately went to the organ, with these word-pictures in my mind, and began to play and sing. The first verse came along with the music, then the second and third verses. Not more than thirty minutes had passed when this hymn, "Beautiful," words and music, was completed.[7]

The song first appeared in 1897 in *Songs of the Evening Light.*

A Child of God

"A Child of God" is a song that has enjoyed great popularity in the Church of God over the years since its first appearance in 1907 in *Truth in Song.* It was born out of an inner conflict in the mind and heart of a young Christian.

In writing about the origin of this song, Warren said

In the early years of my Christian experience, I was struggling to resist the buffetings of Satan who came

A Child of God

"The Spirit himself testifies with our spirit that we are God's children."
—Romans 8:16

11.6.11.6.wR.

Barney E. Warren

CHILD OF GOD
Barney E. Warren

1 Praise the Lord! my heart with His love is beam-ing, I am a child of
2 Let the saints re - joice with my rap - tured spir - it, I am a child of
3 Let a ho - ly life tell the gos - pel sto - ry, I am a child of
4 Saved from sin to - day, ev - ery band is riv - en, I am a child of

1 God; Heav-en's gold-en light o - ver me is stream-ing, I am a child of God.
2 God; I will tes - ti - fy that the world may hear it, I am a child of God.
3 God; How He fills the soul with His grace and glo - ry, I am a child of God.
4 God; Thro' the tests of life I have peace from heav-en, I am a child of God.

I am a child of God, I am a child of God; I have
I am a child, a child of God, I am a child, a child of God;

washed my robes in the cleans-ing foun-tain, I am a child of God.

against me with an accusing attitude. He suggested this thought, "You are not saved; if you were, you would not feel so bad."

Apparently he was determined to overthrow my soul. For my encouragement one of God's promises came quickly to me: "When the enemy shall come in like a flood, the Spirit of the Lord shall lift up a standard against him" (Isa. 59:19).

In this connection I remembered the words that D. S. Warner had spoken regarding the tested promises: "I have so much confidence in God, that I would be willing to hook my little finger over the least of his promises and swing out over the infernal regions, and feel perfectly safe."

Immediately I began to feel more secure as my faith gripped the promise, "God is faithful, who will not suffer you to be tempted above that ye are able; but will with the temptation also make a way to escape, that ye may be able to bear it" (1 Cor. 10:13). I reviewed my consecration carefully, and every cause for doubts cleared away. I resisted Satan steadfastly in the faith proclaiming, "I am a child of God."[8]

Every Hour for Jesus

The song "Every Hour for Jesus" was written during the 1900 Moundsville, West Virginia, camp meeting. Barney Warren had just preached a sermon on making the most of the time in working for the Lord.

In her biography of Warren, Axchie Bolitho said that Warren's sermon came from a burden Warren had for "'messengers' who had no place to deliver themselves of their 'burdens.'" Being a messenger in the early days of the movement meant travel and pioneering, since there were few settled congregations. "But pioneering is difficult and not everyone who felt the call of God upon him could enter new places and get for himself a hearing."[9]

Bolitho recounted that after that camp meeting service, "the pressure on [Warren's] spirit made him seek a quiet place for meditation. There the words and music of this song came together as if the whole were really but one effort. Returning to the camp, Mr. Warren sang the song, from the manuscript, to the evening congregation."[10]
The song first appeared in *Salvation Echoes*, which was published that same year.

Joy Unspeakable

The song "Joy Unspeakable" was first published in the 1900 songbook *Salvation Echoes*. The following story is from the writings of B. E. Warren about the song:

> Some years ago, while I was engaged in a camp meeting in northwestern Ohio, I left the grounds and walked out for prayer and meditation. I found an artesian well. The water was flowing from it with great force in a stream the full size of the pipe.
> I threw a chip into the pipe from which the stream was flowing, but the force of the water was so great that it carried the chip away. I then picked up a large round stick of wood about a foot in length and forced it down the pipe, but the powerful stream quickly brought it up and carried it away.
> This incident reminded me of our Savior's conversation with the woman of Samaria who came to Jacob's well to draw water. [See John 4:5-26.] "Jesus answered. . . . Whosoever drinketh of this water shall thirst again: But whosoever drinketh of the water that I shall give him shall never thirst; but the water that I shall give him shall be in him a well of water springing up into everlasting life" [vv. 13-14].
> Peter expressed this in writing: "Though now ye see him not, yet believing, ye rejoice with joy unspeakable and full of glory" (1 Pet. 1:8).

The highly figurative language of Jesus and of Peter formed the basis for "Joy Unspeakable."[11]

The Kingdom of Peace

The following story is from the writings of B. E. Warren about the song "The Kingdom of Peace."

One day D. S. Warner and I were in conversation with a man about the kingdom of God.

The man said to us, "I am looking for a kingdom to come down from heaven larger than the whole state of Colorado, and I am doing all of the good works that I can, so that I shall be worthy to enter into it when it comes."

In reply, we told him that God's kingdom is not a temporal kingdom but a spiritual kingdom. ("My kingdom is not of this world" [John 18:36]), but a spiritual kingdom. "Neither shall they say, Lo here! or, lo there! for, behold, the kingdom of God is within you" (Luke 17:21). "For the kingdom of God is not meat and drink; but righteousness, and peace, and joy in the Holy Ghost" (Rom. 14:17).

Our conversation, in the use of the Scriptures on the kingdom, gave inspiration and form to this hymn.[12]

The song was first published in *Songs of the Evening Light,* 1897, under the title "What a Kingdom!" Later the title was changed to "The Kingdom of Peace."

Lord, Take the First Place

This song was one of Warren's later works, probably written in the middle 1920s. It first appeared in the *Melodies of Zion* songbook published in 1926. Warren had this to say about the writing of it:

This hymn was born in Charleston, West Virginia. It was in the early morning hours while Mrs. Warren and I were on our knees in family worship.

We were struggling with some real problems which gave us a deeper and more comprehensive vision of consecration. During Mrs. Warren's prayer she pleadingly said, "Lord, take the first place in my heart."

By a touch of inspiration these words were immortalized. Giving God the first place in my heart! It presented a new world of meaning to me. We were up from our knees but a very short time when the hymn was completed.[13]

Press the Battle On

The song "Press the Battle On" likely was written in 1900, the same year it appeared in *Salvation Echoes*. Axchie Bolitho wrote in her biography of Barney Warren the circumstances under which the song was penned:

It was unusually hot and dry the summer young Barney Warren and Charles Naylor held a tent meeting in Hickman's Grove near Meeker in Northwestern Ohio. The deep sand and the heat moved Mr. Warren to pray for rain.

The answer came with a vengeance just after the service had closed one Sunday afternoon. . . . The two young evangelists in their long-tailed coats, the rain streaming off them, struggled to get the tent down before it should be destroyed. Then they took refuge in their sleeping tent. There they lay, without lights, upon their cots while the rain beat upon the tent and streamed down its sides.

Presently Barney began to whistle, improvising as he went. After a moment Charles said: "Keep on whistling, and write this down." Barney, keeping up his competition with the rain, thunder, and lightning, found in his pocket an old envelope and a pencil, and wrote while Charles dictated. . . . Though he could not see the envelope before him in the darkness, he somehow got the words and enough of the tune down so that, when morning came, he was able to finish it.[14]

The River of Peace

This song, which was first published in *Echoes from Glory* in 1893 was written in the 1880s in western Pennsylvania. The story as told by Warren is as follows:

Brother Warner and I had been strolling about in the woods. We sat down on a log to rest just where the Allegheny River makes a curve, giving us a lovely view of the river and of the valley beyond. The beauty of the scene awakened inspiration in both of us. Brother Warner suggested that this constantly flowing river very fittingly represents the continual flow of the river of peace in the soul of the redeemed. When we left that log, both the words and the music of "The River of Peace" were roughly outlined.[15]

Victory

This song was one of Warren's earlier compositions; it was written in 1897 and published that same year in *Songs of the Evening Light.*
Warren told the story behind this song:

It happened during a camp meeting that a very conscientious young man, unfortunately a victim of accusations and doubt, came to the altar of prayer. It was difficult for him to believe that it was his privilege to have the victory in his own soul over Satan and sin. He struggled and prayed until the general altar service had ended. We remained kneeling together. I called his attention to every promise which seemed to me to fit his particular need, but all to no profit.

Finally the Lord called my attention to some scriptures that did bring him help: "This is the victory that overcometh the world, even our faith." I told him that believing is taking God at his Word, that the Lord had bought him with his own blood; that he was not his own, but the Lord's. I insisted that a man can use his will to believe the same as he can use his feet to walk or his hands to handle. Presently the young man rose from the altar, a glow of joy on his face, and with rejoicing, he said, "The victory is mine!"

In this hymn, I have tried to express the wonder of an experience of God's grace which brings real victory to those who trust in the Lord and stand on his Word. It is the testimony type of song, and one that describes the experience of many of God's true children.[16]

Will You Come?

The song came about during a revival meeting B. E. Warren and his brother, William, were conducting in Darke County, Ohio. Warren says this:

> Though we were in the country, we were in close proximity to three or four small towns and the county seat. The meeting progressed with success and increasing crowds. The Lord was present in the power of conviction and saving grace.
>
> One evening during an altar service, a young convert was so overjoyed in his soul and so blessed that he became deeply burdened for others. He arose and exhorted in the Spirit, saying, "Will you come to Jesus; oh, will you come?"
>
> These simple words struck me with unusual inspiration. After the altar service was ended, I withdrew to a small tent and wrote both words and music with ease. I

Barney E. Warren as a young man

wrote the song with an earnest prayer that God would make it a blessing to many hearts and that it would encourage them to surrender to Him.[17]

The song first appeared in *Truth in Song* in the year 1907.

J. W. Byers in younger years

4

Jacob W. Byers:

Pioneer Minister to the West Coast

Jacob Whistler Byers made his entrance into the world on March 26, 1859, at Albany, Illinois. He grew up on a farm and became a school teacher. In a Methodist revival held in 1876, Byers was converted, but drifted from his faith for a while after that.

Jacob's father had been preaching in both English and German with a church group known as the River Brethren, when in the early 1880s, he learned about the *Gospel Trumpet* and subscribed to it. The elder Byers began to preach holiness, which brought on persecution from some River Brethren leaders.

Meanwhile J. W. had made a recommitment to Christ, had married Jennie M. Shirk, and had begun preaching in the River Brethren church. He claimed the experience of sanctification in 1884. When the Byers family met D. S. Warner and his company in 1888, J. W. and his father were ordained into the ministry with the Church of God reformation movement.

After two years in evangelistic work in Illinois, Jacob and Jennie and their three children packed up and traveled to the West Coast to preach the gospel there. They arrived in San Diego, California, in November 1890. In a letter to the *Trumpet* early in 1891, the Byerses had this to say about their work: "We are just beginning to realize the stupendous work there is to be done here, and why God saw fit to separate us from our dear ones for the work on the coast. Oh, how we appreciate the prayers of the dear saints."[1]

J. W. and Jennie were active in city mission work in San Diego and Los Angeles for some six years. Then in 1896 they moved to Oakland, where they opened a healing home mission and published a magazine called *Tidings of Healing.* The Byerses were put in charge of the missionary home in Oakland in 1906. J. W. did some pastoral work in Oakland also, while Jennie led a sewing circle that worked on behalf of missions.

C. E. Brown, later *Gospel Trumpet* editor, traveled with J. W. Byers in evangelistic work in California, Oregon, and Washington in 1904. He wrote that Byers "was a man of stainless honor. . . . He had what is as nearly as conceivable a complete blending of the apparently contradictory traits of dignity and humility. He was never feverish in activity, yet he never grew cold."[2]

This Byers brother seems to have written few published songs, but he wrote articles for the *Gospel Trumpet* and tracts. He also authored some books, among them *Grace of Healing, Bible Humility,* and *Parent and Child.*

Jacob W. Byers died October 16, 1944, at the age of 85. He and Jennie had pastored a number of churches in California, and "were regarded by all who knew them as a real father and mother to the churches," wrote California minister L. W. Guilford. "To the last [Byers] was sound in all the truths of the reformation, and his vision of the church was as clear as the noonday sun."[3]

He Is Just the Same Today

"He Is Just the Same Today," which first appeared in 1897 in *Songs of the Evening Light,* was the result of efforts of the two Byers brothers, Jacob and Andrew.

Many of the words of the song relate to healing. Jacob W. Byers believed in Jesus' continued power to heal. He was "very much burdened with the ministry of healing," Editor C. E. Brown later wrote about Byers, "and he and Jennie opened a healing home in the city of Oakland in 1896. Many wonderful cases of healing accompanied their ministry during the two-and-a-half years this home continued, as well as at other times in their work."[4]

Andrew L. Byers, who composed the music to the song and helped prepare the 1897 songbook in which the song appeared, remembered specific circumstances about his contribution to this song. "The words had a rhythm very similar to another song on the same subject," he said, "and one evening I tired myself trying to compose a tune not too much like the other song. It seemed I could accomplish nothing, so I gave it up and retired. Next morning the new tune was in my very waking thoughts."[5]

J. W. Byers and family (about 1910)

31

He Is Just the Same Today

"Jesus Christ is the same yesterday and today and forever."—Hebrews 13:8

Based on Hebrews 13:8
Jacob W. Byers

THE SAME TODAY
Andrew L. Byers

1 Have you ev - er heard of Je - sus, How He came from heav'n to earth
2 Do you see the peo - ple gath - er 'Round that great and ho - ly Man,
3 Is it true that ev - 'ry sick-ness May be laid at Je-sus' feet?
4 O that pre - cious, lov - ing Je - sus! His com - pas-sion still the same

1 With a name of might - y vir - tue, Tho' by ver - y hum-ble birth?
2 Bring-ing all the sick and suf-f'ring, Com-ing to Him all who can?
3 All my trou-ble, care, and sor - row, And I rest in joy com-plete?
4 For each sin - ful, suf - f'ring mor - tal Who seeks re - fuge in His name.

1 When the world was held in bond-age Un - der Sa - tan's dis - mal sway,
2 See Him look with great com-pas-sion As they faint-ed by the way!
3 Yes, my friend, in ev - 'ry sad-ness, If by faith to Him you pray,
4 Heed the pre - sent in - vi - ta - tion, O you need not stay a - way!

1 Je - sus healed their dread dis-eas - es— He is just the same to - day.
2 How He called them gent - ly to Him! He is just the same to - day.
3 He'll re - move with ten - der mer - cy, For He's just the same to - day.
4 Come, re - ceive His heal-ing fa - vor, For He's just the same to - day.

32

He is just the same to - day,
He is just the same to-day, just the same to-day,

He is just the same to - day (the same to - day);
He is just the same to-day, just the same to - day,

Yes, He healed in Gal - li - lee, Set the suf - f'ring cap - tives free,

And He's just the same to - day. (the same to - day).
And He's just the same, He is just the same to - day.

And He's just the same, the same to - day.

33

A. L. Byers

5

Andrew L. Byers:
A Composer of Tunes

When Andrew L. Byers was born in 1869, it was into a family fond of and gifted in music. His early recollections included regular family worship, which many times involved the singing of hymns. When Byers was eight or nine, his father gave him his first music reading lesson.

Though Byers developed a love for music early in life, he did not think of trying his hand at music composition until D. S. Warner and his group of singers visited the Byers' family home in Illinois in April 1888. Of this meeting Byers wrote: "Perhaps I should never have started in tune composition had I not met Bro. B. E. Warren. . . . He was but a youth, as was I. He and Brother Warner were preparing the book *Anthems from the Throne*.

"When I saw Brother Barney at the organ, actually working on original composition and putting it on paper, I thought it was wonderful. But the religious movement which they represented was charged with heavenly song, and somehow it wanted to work out through me also."[1] That year Byers composed his first tune to words written by his sister; the song was published in the new songbook.

Byers had been teaching in Iowa, but in June 1891 he came to work with the Trumpet Family, then located in Grand Junction, Michigan. His future wife, Della Wickersham, arrived at the Trumpet office the same day.

In 1898 the Trumpet Family, now in Moundsville, West Virginia, was officially incorporated into the Gospel Trumpet Company. Andrew Byers was a charter member of the board of directors. He served as vice-president of the company for thirty-three years.

During his years as a Gospel Trumpet Company employee (1891-1922), Byers served twenty years as managing editor of the *Trumpet*. After that he became book editor and was in charge of the information department. He was involved in the editing of every hymnal and songbook published by the company from 1897 until 1936—some eleven of them.

In addition to writing music, Byers wrote books and articles dealing with Church of God history. In 1907 he wrote *The Gospel Trumpet Publishing Work: Described and Illustrated*, a book describing the origin and operations of the company. In 1920, a series of biographical sketches "Pioneers of the Present Reformation" appeared in the *Gospel Trumpet*. Then in 1921 he wrote a major book about the life of D. S. Warner called *Birth of a Reformation*. These publications may have prompted Editor Charles E. Brown in 1951 to describe Andrew Byers as "a historian of this movement."[2]

Though he is most remembered as a music composer, Byers himself did not feel he had given as much time to his composing as he would have liked. "Song writing," he wrote, "for the greater part of my life at the Gospel Trumpet Office was not a constant thing. It was only in connection with a new book proposed that I would get started. This was due to the absorbing work in the Publishing Office. My tunes are therefore comparatively few—only about two hundred fifty in a period of thirty-eight years."[3]

In 1922 the Byers family left the Gospel Trumpet Company and moved to California, where they helped develop various local congregations. Andrew Byers died on November 9, 1952, at the age of eighty-two, after a prolonged illness.

Because He Loves Me

Some songs were easier to compose than others, according to A. L. Byers. This song, which first appeared in *Songs of Grace and Glory* in 1918, was such a one.

Byers said, "One Sunday evening before attending service at Park Place Church in Anderson, Indiana, I sat down to the piano, having before me the song poem 'Because He Loves Me' by C. W. Naylor. The reverie of the words possessed me, and this, together with the rhythm suggesting a triple-measure swing, almost made the tune. Never did words more nearly sing themselves."[4]

I'm on the Winning Side

The song "I'm on the Winning Side" appeared for the first time in the songbook *Reformation Glory* in 1923. The songbook was advertised as "a new and inspiring collection of gospel hymns for evangelistic services." It was a less expensive, less bulky songbook for use in evangelistic services than *Select Hymns*, which had been produced in 1911.

At the time of the song's birth, the two writers were already well-known in Church of God circles. Charles W. Naylor was a frequently used writer in the *Gospel Trumpet* and had written more than eighty published song poems. Andrew L. Byers had written the historical book *Birth of a Reformation* and more than two hundred song tunes.

Though not himself a writer of song lyrics, with this song Byers was able to prompt someone else to write the words. In explaining how the song came about, he wrote, "I listened to a brother preach who said something about being on the winning side. Instantly this suggested itself as a title for a song. The suggestion was passed on to Brother Naylor and he composed the words. Then one Fourth of July, while sitting by a tree in a cemetery, I worked out the tune."[5]

Listed under the topic "Victory" in the 1923 songbook's index, the song has the feel of a triumphant march.

When My King Shall Call for Me

"So he called ten of his servants and gave them ten minas. 'Put this money to work,' he said, 'until I come back.'" —Luke 19:13

Lizzie DeArmond

WHEN MY KING SHALL CALL
Andrew L. Byers

1 With a hap-py song I will haste a-long, In His serv - ice faith - ful be;
2 In the val-ley deep, on the moun-tain steep, Tho His face I can - not see,
3 He will hold me fast to the ver - y last, For a tow'r of strength is He;
4 In a cheer-y way let me toil each day, Help-ing oth - ers lov - ing - ly,

1 All the things that fret I shall soon for-get, When my King shall call for me.
2 With a pur - pose true all His will I'll do, Till my King shall call for me.
3 So I'll sing His praise thru the long, long days, When my King shall call for me.
4 With my work well done at the set of sun, When my King shall call for me.

May He find me in my place When my King shall call for me;
May He find me in my place When my King shall call for me;

With a loy-al heart do-ing well my part When my King shall call for me.

When My King Shall Call for Me

"When My King Shall Call for Me" first appeared in the 1920s in *Hymns and Spiritual Songs.* About the author of the words, we know little. According to the *Dictionary of American Hymnology,* Lizzie DeArmond was a member of the Presbyterian Church and lived in Pennsylvania. She wrote several song poems that were picked up by other church groups. She may have been one of those persons who submitted their unsolicited poems to the Gospel Trumpet Company for possible publication.

Andrew Byers, who composed the music, was also one of the music editors for the new hymn book. He may have gone through a stack of poetry contributions, found Lizzie DeArmond's poem, liked it, and set it to music. He was living and pastoring in Harrisburg, Oregon, in 1924 when he set the words to music.

Byers evidently was asked occasionally how he composed. His answer was, "Well, one endeavors to think out a tune just as one tries to think what to say when writing a letter. He just composes, that is all, and writes it down; and if he is inspired to say something good, he just says it."[6] Then he went on to describe how he studied the words for the musical setting, rhythm, and measure.

W. Dale Oldham wrote of Byers that his "work was solidly and thoroughly done. . . . He was not a poet but was an excellent judge of poetry. . . . His own music is mature and of a nature to endure."[7]

W. J. Henry and wife

6

William J. Henry:
Zealous in Spreading the Gospel

William J. Henry was born on December 2, 1867, in Ohio. He became a Christian in 1882 during an evangelistic meeting held in Jerry City in the home of Mother Sarah Smith, who became one of D. S. Warner's traveling company of singers. That meeting was conducted by Warner and A. J. Kilpatrick. At that time Henry took his stand with the Church of God.

Entering the ministry in 1891, Henry became, as John W. V. Smith called him, "one of the most prominent of the 'flying messengers' of the pioneer days."[1]

Henry had been holding evangelistic meetings in the New England area in 1893, when he felt called to go overseas with the gospel. He wrote in a report to the *Gospel Trumpet*, "When we last reported we expected to go to Mass. and N.H. . . . but the Lord has now shown me that he would have me go to the foreign fields, so I humbly submit to his divine will."[2]

In the company of another evangelist, G. R. Achor, Henry set sail for Liverpool, England, on January 7. This trip marked the beginning of Church of God activity in spreading the gospel overseas. Henry held meetings in Liverpool and the surrounding area until October, when he returned to the United States. By that time a small church seems to have begun and three other ministers had come from the United States to carry on the work.

Sometime in the late 1890s, Henry and some others became involved in the "anti-cleansing heresy," also known as Zinzendorfism. This view held that "a person was completely cleansed from sin [including the sinful nature] in the experience of justification [salvation], since Christ's redeeming work was not partial."[3] Therefore, sanctification was not needed for cleansing. This view went against what the Church of God was teaching.

After a time, Henry began to see the view as false and in a letter to the *Trumpet* in June 1900, he renounced the doctrine and asked forgiveness. He was prayed for in the Moundsville, West Virginia, camp meeting soon after and found acceptance by his Church of God brothers and sisters.

Having weathered this low time in his life, Henry came back with renewed zeal in spreading the gospel. He went to Springfield, Missouri, and started a church, which he pastored for thirteen years. He also built a missionary home there. Not limiting himself to one location, he began evangelizing the south central part of Missouri, holding meetings in various places.

Henry's evangelistic zeal carried over into his song poems. He wrote words such as "I'll follow Jesus all the way," and "Souls around you, my brother, are groping in sin,/ Is it nothing to you? Is it nothing to you?/ Surely some of them you may be able to win,/ Is it nothing, nothing to you?"

Henry numbered his songs at more than three hundred. Many of these were never included in a Church of God songbook or hymnal, though some were published in the *Gospel Trumpet*. Two of them, "I Cannot Be Idle" and "Let the Fire Fall on Me," have survived to be included in the newest Church of God hymnal.

Toledo, Ohio, became Henry's permanent address after his Missouri pastorate. He served as pastor to several churches in the area through the years and also conducted evangelistic work in other places such as Indiana, Michigan, and Canada.

Even in his later life, Henry seemed to retain a zeal to

spread the gospel. He and his wife wrote in 1935, "To God be all the glory! This has been the busiest and happiest time of our lives. We are both enjoying the best of health and are decided to do more for [God] in the future."[4] W. J. Henry died October 26, 1955, at the age of 87.

The Love of God

Deeper than the depths of ocean,
Wider than the boundless sea,
Higher than the lofty mountains
Is the love of God to me.
Filled with all his glorious fullness,
Sitting at his blessed feet,
Doing only as he bids me,
This is all my drink and meat.
You may have these earthly pleasures,
You may have earth's fame and store,
I have found a richer treasure,
One that satisfies me more;
In God's love I find completeness,
And an everlasting rest,
Joy that passeth understanding,
Where my soul is ever blest.

—"The Love of God" by W. J. Henry, *Gospel Trumpet* (March 9, 1911), 3.

I Cannot Be Idle

In January 1907 the word went out that a new songbook was to be published for the Church of God in the next several months. The editors already had a large number of songs on hand but still gave an invitation through the *Gospel Trumpet* that any reader wishing to send in words, music, or both might do so for consideration.

I Cannot Be Idle

*"Ask the Lork of the harvest, therefore, to send out workers
into His harvest field."—Matthew 9:38*

William J. Henry

I CANNOT BE IDLE
William J. Henry

1 I can - not be i - dle, for Je - sus says, "Go And
2 I can - not be i - dle, the fields are so white. And
3 I can - not be i - dle, soon time will be o'er, And
4 I can - not be i - dle, no time for re - pose, My

1 work in my har - vest to - day; And then at the eve - ning when
2 num - ber - less sheaves will be lost; They per - ish for want of more
3 reap - ing be end - ed for aye; I'll gath - er the lost from the
4 rest - ing shall be o - ver there, Where all of the faith - ful in

1 la - bor is done, What - ev - er is right I will pay."
2 reap - ers to save— How aw - ful to think of the cost!
3 by - ways of sin To walk in the beau - ti - ful way.
4 heav - en a - bove A crown of bright glo - ry shall wear.

Then a - way to the work I will go And
(I'll go)

44

join in the reap-ing of grain, And back from the har-vest with (I'll go,) beau-ti-ful sheaves I'll come with re-joic-ing a - gain.

W. J. Henry's song "I Cannot Be Idle" might have been among those new compositions sent to the editors in answer to that invitation. The editors chose to include the selection in *Truth in Song,* and it has been included in every major Church of God hymnal since.

No record has been found of a particular incident that may have caused Henry to write this song. We do have record of a turbulent time in his life several years earlier when he had begun to doubt a particular doctrine held firmly by the Church of God. He came through that time with restored faith and a renewed zeal and urgency to be about his Master's business. "I Cannot Be Idle" expresses that zeal and urgency.

C. W. Naylor

7

Charles W. Naylor:
The Singing Heart

"Adversity is quite certain to come to us in one form or another," wrote C. W. Naylor. "We may expect our share and should not leave it out of account in life's plans. . . . We ought to be ready to meet it bravely, confidently, and resourcefully, so that we shall not be overwhelmed."[1]

Naylor was acquainted with adversity. For forty years he wrote songs, books, and articles from his bed. His writings carried words of comfort to others facing adversity.

In 1874, Charles Wesley Naylor was born in Ohio. His mother died when he was eight years old, and he went to live with his grandparents. He was converted in the Methodist church in 1892.

Naylor was introduced to the Church of God that year through a meeting held by evangelists B. E. Warren and S. L. Speck. The evangelists returned to that area the next year, and soon after, Naylor withdrew from the Methodist church to fellowship with the Church of God congregation there.

The Gospel Trumpet Company was still located in Grand Junction when Naylor first came there in 1896. Over the next few years he alternately joined with other ministers to hold evangelistic meetings and worked at the Trumpet office. He was the first pastor in Columbus, Ohio, staying about five months.

In August 1907 he began an evangelistic tour through the southern United States. While helping to remove some timbers under the tent at a meeting in Sidney, Florida, in 1908, Naylor was injured seriously, dislocating one kidney. A short while later he was injured again in a bus accident and took to his bed in June 1909, where he remained the rest of his life.

Naylor came from a literary family. His father wrote poetry and a cousin was a novelist and columnist. Another cousin was a song writer. Naylor wrote many songs and much prose. As C. E. Brown wrote about his literary efforts: "Naylor wrote continuously for the *Gospel Trumpet* for many years, besides writing eight books, many tracts and pamphlets, and one hundred fifty gospel songs."[2]

Among Naylor's writings was the book *The Secret of the Singing Heart,* which was also tape recorded for the blind. In that book Naylor wrote, "The secret of the singing heart consists in learning to be what we ought to be and in holding the attitude we ought to hold toward life. It consists in learning to adjust ourselves to our circumstances and to be happy in those circumstances. . . . It consists in walking with God, believing in him, and acting out that belief day by day. Doing this we shall ever be blessed."[3]

Charles W. Naylor died February 21, 1950. Though an invalid, he had walked with God and was a source of encouragement for many.

An Excerpt from *When Adversity Comes:*

It was a cold winter morning. Snow covered the ground. The frost on the trees sparkled in the bright sunlight like ten thousand diamonds. But the brightness outside seemed to find no reflection in me. I had been confined to my bed for more than six months. I was gloomy and despondent. It seemed as though all the light and joy had gone out of my life and that only pain and suffering and sorrow were left to me. I had no desire to live. Again and again I prayed that I might die. I should have welcomed any form of death. I had grown morbid and was almost in despair. I had been prayed for again and again, but the healing touch came not. Life seemed to hold for me no ray of hope, no gleam of sunshine.

As I lay brooding in my melancholy state a cardinal, in his bright red plumage, alighted on a tree a few feet from my window. His eyes sparkled as he gazed at me with interest. He turned his head now this way and now that, apparently studying me intently, and then he gave me a cheery call and hopped as near to me as he could get and repeated his cries over and over. Somehow his cries took the form of word in my mind. This is what he said to me: 'You, you, you, cheer up! Cheer up! Cheer up!'

For more than two hours he continued to repeat this, and then went away. Far in the distance I heard the last echoes of his notes still saying, "Cheer up! Cheer up!"

It seemed as though God had sent the bird to bring a message to my soul. . . . I began to think over the favorable side of my situation. I began to consider how many things the Lord had bestowed upon me in the past—his mercy, his kindness, and his blessings. My heart took courage.

—From *When Adversity Comes* by C. W. Naylor, (Anderson, IN: Gospel Trumpet Company, 1944), 138-140.

I Am the Lord's

One of our heritage songs that has given many people comfort and help over the years is "I Am the Lord's," which first appeared in *Truth in Song*, 1907. Charles Naylor gave the following account of its writing:

When this song was written, I had been out of the ministry a number of months taking care of my grandfather, who had been seriously injured. I was sitting by the window, watching the raindrops as they were falling rapidly. I was feeling rather discouraged

I Am the Lord's, I Know

"Who shall separate us from the love of Christ? Shall trouble or hardship or persecution or famine or nakedness or danger or sword?"—Romans 8:35

Based on Romans 8:35-39
Charles W. Naylor

I AM THE LORD'S
D. Otis Teasley

1 Wheth-er I live or die, Wheth-er I wake or sleep,
2 When with a-bun-dant store Or in deep pov-er-ty,
3 When I am safe at home Or in a for-eign land,
4 Noth-ing shall sep-a-rate From His un-bound-ed love,

1 Wheth-er up-on the land Or on the storm-y deep;
2 And when the world may smile Or it may frown on me;
3 When on an ice-bound shore Or on a sun-lit strand;
4 Nei-ther in depths be-low Nor in the heights a-bove;

1 When 'tis se-rene and calm Or when the wild winds blow,
2 When it shall help me on Or shall ob-struct my way,
3 When on the moun-tain height Or in the val-ley low,
4 And in the years to come He will a-bide with me;

rit.

1 I shall not be a-fraid— I am the Lord's, I know.
2 Still shall my heart re-joice— I am the Lord's to-day.
3 Still doth He care for me— I am the Lord's, I know.
4 I am the Lord's, I know, For all e-ter-ni-ty.

because I could not be in the work and because it seemed that there were no opportunities in that place for usefulness or to work for the Lord in any way.

Finally in my meditation I thought, Well, if I can do nothing, I am the Lord's anyway. As I thought over this fact my heart warmed with gratitude to the Lord. I took my pencil and paper and began to express the feelings that were in my heart as nearly as I could in the words of the song.

It seemed more an act of worship than an act of authorship, and with it came a sense of comfort, of trustful security, and a deep sense of God's Fatherhood and care.[4]

Sin Can Never Enter There

The song "Sin Can Never Enter There" was written sometime in February 1899, according to the poet C. W. Naylor. These were the early days of Naylor's ministry. The occasion was a revival meeting in Sandusky County, Ohio, at which both Naylor and B. E. Warren were leaders. Naylor wrote about the circumstances surrounding the song's birth:

The meeting began in an old house which had had the partitions knocked out and had been seated for the meeting. The weather was extremely cold, the coldest I ever experienced. At the afternoon service Brother Warren preached. He had previously spoken of this subject, but while he was preaching, it was so forcibly impressed upon my mind that I wrote the song while he was preaching.

On our way back to our stopping place I showed [the song] to [Warren]. Arriving there, he sat down at the organ and in a short time had the tune for it. Then we all sang it together.

The meeting was later moved to a church-building, which was crowded night after night, even in the worst of weather, until finally the roads became impassable. Several souls were saved in the meeting, and the church was much encouraged.[5]

The song first appeared in the 1900 songbook *Salvation Echoes.*

8

Clarence E. Hunter:
Building Churches and Writing Music

Clarence E. Hunter was born in 1869. He entered the ministry in 1892 and began traveling with D. S. Warner on evangelistic tours. Clarence Hunter could sing, and Warner had evidently liked Hunter's voice enough to ask him to join him. Music was an important part of the meetings.

At a Grand Junction, Michigan, camp meeting, Hunter met Nora Siens. She was also a minister. The two were married in the fall of 1896 at Cedardale Chapel near Federalsburg, Maryland, where Nora and Lena Shoffner had helped to start a congregation.

The Hunters traveled for a while, holding evangelistic meetings. They pastored in Kansas, Indiana, Pennsylvania, and California, in many places building up new congregations. At times Nora pastored the church while Clarence went to work with his hands to support the family and help support these new congregations. One such time was in San Diego, California, where Clarence worked in a shipyard.

Not only did Clarence Hunter sing and do the work of a pioneer minister; he also composed music. He wrote tunes for songwriters D. S. Warner, B. E. Warren, C. E. Orr, W. G. Schell, Clara McAlister Brooks, and C. W. Naylor. Some of his tunes appeared as early as 1897 in the Church of God songbook *Songs of the Evening Light*.

In 1899 he wrote an article in the *Gospel Trumpet* to readers who were "blessed with a talent for writing poetry." He said, "I have no special gift of poetry, but would love to

Clarence Hunter (with Nora and son Paul)

have some good words, as I am preparing to write music. I would like to have some good words for children's meetings, about three verses in a song. . . . I ask the prayers of all the dear saints that I may be able to accomplish what God wants me to learn in music."[1]

Hunter was instrumental in the compiling of the 1900 songbook *Salvation Echoes* for the Gospel Trumpet Company; he worked with B. E. Warren, D. O. Teasley, and A. L. Byers. More than thirty of Hunter's hymn tunes were included in that volume.

When a new songbook *Truth in Song* was being compiled in 1907, Hunter was again a part of the editing work force. In this volume two songs appeared for the first time with words by Naylor and music by Hunter that are still in use today: "God's Way Is Best" and "My Heart Says Amen."

Hunter lived to his mid-seventies, having fought with ill health many of those later years. He died in August 1945.

My Heart Says Amen

The song "My Heart Says Amen" dates back to the 1907 songbook *Truth in Song*, published by the Gospel Trumpet Company. The writers of the words and music, Charles W. Naylor and Clarence E. Hunter, both worked in putting together that book.

In the October 19, 1922, issue of the *Gospel Trumpet*, Naylor explained how the words came to be written:

> I had been out of the ministry for a time because of the serious ill health of a member of our family, which required my attendance upon him. I had been passing through a time of sore conflict and deep trial. I had faced a situation that had required all the strength of my manhood to meet successfully. It had seemed to demand the giving up of all my plans and hopes, and the making of a sacrifice than which none could be greater.
>
> I had not rebelled against the will of the Lord, but had sought to fully reconcile myself to it. This was, I suppose, the greatest battle ever fought in my life—not simply to submit to God, for I had that settled all the way along. The problem was to submit and be satisfied and contented in the submission.
>
> I finally reached the point where I was perfectly contented with God's will, no matter what it might require of me. After a few days of sweet soul-rest which resulted from complete yielding, the inspiration to write this song came upon me, and in a little while it was completed.[2]

Clarence Hunter surely knew this kind of "giving up of all plans and hopes." He and his wife had lost their one-year-old twins in the summer of 1903. Shortly after their deaths, an item appeared in the *Gospel Trumpet* (September 3, 1903), written by the Hunters. It read, "While we miss our

55

My Heart Says Amen

"Yet, not as I will, but as you will."—Matthew 26:39c

Charles W. Naylor

MY HEART SAYS AMEN
Clarence E. Hunter

1 I have yield-ed my-self to Thy serv-ice, And Thy pres-ence my
2 All the heart-ties of earth may be sun-dered, So that I may Thy
3 Tho my plans and my hopes may seem blight-ed, I will love Thee and
4 When I pass to that heav-en-ly coun-try, And my soul with its

1 soul Thou doth fill; O my Sav-ior, I haste to o-bey Thee, And my
2 pur-pose ful-fill; Help me glad-ly sub-mit and not mur-mur, Ev-er
3 trust in Thee still, For I know all is well that Thou do-est, And my
4 glo-ry doth thrill,This for-ev-er shall be my re-joic-ing, That my

1 heart says a-men to Thy will.
2 say-ing a-men to Thy will.
3 heart says a-men to Thy will.
4 heart said a-men to Thy will.

Yes, my heart says a-men to Thy

will, Lord, And I know that Thou lov-est me still, While I bow low in

hum - ble sub - mis - sion, And my heart says a-men to Thy will.

darlings, yet from our hearts we can say, 'The Lord gave, and the Lord hath taken away; blessed be the name of the Lord.' "[3]

"My Heart Says Amen" is a song of submission, speaking to a question that all who are serious about following Christ must face. It seems that the two men who brought this song to birth more than eighty years ago had experienced this question of wills in their lives, and had learned to say, "My heart says amen to thy will, Lord."

D. O. Teasley

9

D. Otis Teasley:
A Man of Many Talents

"D. O. Teasley was a man of extraordinary natural abilities," wrote Charles E. Brown in his book *When the Trumpet Sounded.* "He speedily took a leading place among ministers."[1] Teasley, who was born in 1876 and entered the ministry of the Church of God in 1896, served in an unusual variety of endeavors—and excelled in each one.

In 1904 Daniel Otis Teasley and his wife, Ora, took charge of the work of establishing a missionary home in New York City.

The New York City missionary home came into being, to a great extent, because of D. O. Teasley's answer to a call he felt God had on his life. "For some time," he wrote in January 1904, "I have felt led of the Lord to move to New York City and open up a missionary home. . . . I feel now that it is God's will to have us move to New York in the fall of the present year, and I ask all God's people to pray that we may move in God's order."[2]

The home was in a rented facility when the Teasleys came. By 1908 they were able to establish a permanent location on Grand Avenue. The home remained at that location until it ceased operation.

One of Teasley's better-known talents was his song writing. He composed the music to more than eighty songs. For at least thirty of these, he wrote the words, also. Some of these songs are still sung today. He worked as one of the editors of several of the songbooks published by the Gospel Trumpet Company: *Salvation Echoes* (1900), *Truth in Song*

(1907), *Select Hymns* (1911), and *Songs of Grace and Glory* (1918).

In his book *Giants Along My Path*, W. Dale Oldham wrote of Teasley and his talent for song writing: "I think he was probably the best all-round songwriter among us. Teasley not only knew the rules of harmony and used them correctly and creatively, he also was able to teach and communicate those basics to others."[3]

Teasley was a teacher, not only of music, but of the Bible, holding Bible classes for Gospel Trumpet Family members as early as 1910. By 1917, he had taught a Bible geography class that was so popular that the notes were revised and worked into a book: *Historical Geography of the Bible.*

The Gospel Trumpet Company came to know of Teasley's talents in finance and administration. During part of 1903-1904, while Editor E. E. Byrum was on a trip around the world, Teasley managed company finances.

Later, in 1910, the company was promoting Sunday school and the need for curriculum resources. D. O. Teasley was on the job, promoting the Sunday school through traveling to churches and through writings in the *Gospel Trumpet*. In 1911, he wrote a book called *How to Conduct a Sunday School*, perhaps this movement's first Christian leadership resource specifically dealing with Sunday school.

After an absence of about five years, when he pastored a church in Alabama and worked in business, Teasley returned to the Gospel Trumpet Company in 1917 to chair the Board of Directors and become general manager of all departments.

The years 1917-1919 were transitional years for the Gospel Trumpet Company. One big change was to begin giving salaries to employees. Until this time workers at the company volunteered their labor—receiving only room and board and a small expense allowance. "D. O. Teasley did much of the work on the early planning for this change," wrote Harold L. Phillips in his history of the company. "He became general manager in June 1917, and had the new plan operational in September."[4]

Soon after these transition years, D. O. Teasley dropped out of sight. Oldham explained it this way: "D. O. Teasley disappeared from the scene . . . because of a time of discouragement which came out of his relationships with some of our executive group. I don't know much of the story or who was at fault, but I have always thought it a shame that a man so talented was not given better understanding from his brethren. We are so quick to censure and so slow to encourage. Be that as it may, Teasley dropped out of church work for a number of years, making a living through the use of yet another talent, commercial art.

"We lost track of him for awhile but finally heard that he had again found a satisfactory relationship with the Lord."[5]

D. O. Teasley—author, songwriter, Christian educator, administrator—died in 1942. But in those years of active service, he made valuable contributions to the Church of God movement and God's kingdom.

Eternity

I stood at the time-beaten portals,
Where many a pilgrim had passed
Out into the infinite future,
To be with the pure and the blest;
And musing in silent devotion,
Eternity seemed to draw near,
And strains from the choir of the faithful
I seemed in my fancy to hear.

I lingered and silently listened
To the dull, heavy tread of the years,
And thought of the fate of the guilty
When Christ in his glory appears.
A shudder came over my spirit

As I thought what a moment might cost;
For eternity's stillness was broken
By the groans and the sighs of the lost.

I saw then the Judge in his splendor,
As he stepped to his great judgment-seat,
And thought of the crashing of ages,
When Time and Eternity meet:
For Time, who has laid many millions
To slumber in death's silent shade,
Shall reel at Eternity's presence,
And sleep in the tomb he has made.

Let us work while 'tis day, brother, sister;
For soon shall the Master return
To garner the wheat that we harvest,
The chaff in his fury to burn.
Then, in haste let us rush to the rescue,
But few can we save at the most:
Soon millions shall be at the judgment,
Forever eternally lost.

— "Eternity" by D. O. Teasley, from *Treasures of Poetry* (Anderson, IN: Gospel Trumpet Company, 1913), 335-36. Also set to music.

A Song of Joy

"A Song of Joy" first appeared in the songbook *Salvation Echoes*, dating it at around 1900. Teasley, the songwriter, had entered the ministry four years earlier.

About the writing of the song, Teasley had this to say:

Though it may seem like a paradox, the hymn "A Song of Joy" was written at a time when I was passing through the deepest sorrow that, up to that time, I had undergone. The event that had caused my sorrow was

A Song of Joy

"Speak to one another with psalms, hymns and spiritual songs. Sing and make music in your heart to the Lord."—Ephesians 5:19

D. Otis Teasley

SONG OF JOY
D. Otis Teasley

1 Sal - va-tion's free, glad joy to all Of Ad - am's fall -en race;
2 From wells of ev - er - last-ing joy Our strength by faith we bring;
3 How blest the soul that's purged as pure As gold with-out al - loy!
4 I'll live for Christ thru this dark world, And faith-ful I will be;

1 We'll tell the sto - ry far and near Of sav - ing, keep-ing grace.
2 The joy that thrills my ran-somed soul Can make the sad heart sing.
3 How peace-ful is the flow - ing stream Of deep e - ter - nal joy!
4 The joy I know that keeps my soul Shall last e - ter - nal - ly.

There's joy, glad joy Now flow -ing from a - bove;
There's joy, glad joy, there's joy, glad joy

There's joy, glad joy In the full-ness of His love.
There's joy, glad joy, there's joy, glad joy

the death of my dear mother.

The thought of the hymn was inspired by the admonition in James, the first chapter and the second verse: "Count it all joy." My determination to find and to hold a higher joy than those derived from early sources and to"live for Christ through this dark world," found expression in the words of "A Song of Joy."

Greater sorrows than I experienced at that time have since been mine; and at times, my joy-light has almost gone out, but my determination to "live for Christ through this dark world" and to be "faithful" are still unbroken.[6]

Back to the Blessed Old Bible

When his song "Back to the Blessed Old Bible" came out in *Truth in Song* in 1907, Teasley was helping establish a missionary home in New York City. He recorded the circumstances around the writing of this song:

This hymn was written on a boat as I was coming down Long Island Sound from Providence, R.I., to my home in New York City. I had just closed a successful meeting in Boston, held in company with other workers, and the nature of the meeting required frequent preaching on doctrinal subjects.

The power of the truth as it is revealed in the Bible, the triumph of the fundamentals as we know and teach them, and the victories of the meeting just closed generated a joy in my soul that sang itself out in the words.[7]

10

William H. Oldham:
Farmer, Preacher, Composer

William Harrison Oldham was born on a farm near Rose Hill, Kansas, on August 19,1875. Later the family moved to what was then Indian territory in Ripley, Oklahoma. When Oldham was nineteen, some Church of God evangelists came to the area and began holding services in a schoolhouse. William, his brothers John and George, and his sister Mattie all accepted the teachings of the Church of God.

Oldham married Myrtle Elmore in 1897 in Ripley. To this union, four children were born, one of whom was W. Dale, who later became a well-known pastor as well as the first speaker for the "Christian Brotherhood Hour" radio program.

At some point during this time, W. H. Oldham felt the call to the ministry and began serving right there in Ripley. "After 1900 when the railroad went through, Ripley started growing, and in 1901 Church of God services began in the town, with W. H. Oldham the first pastor."[1]

During his forty-eight years in the ministry, he served pastorates in Ripley, Oklahoma; Clinton, Iowa; Indianapolis, Huntington, North Webster, and Rushville, Indiana; Hickory, North Carolina; and Stanford, Illinois. A tribute printed in the Gospel Trumpet after his death said that Oldham preached the truth "without fanaticism and without compromise."[2]

According to son, Dale, W. H. Oldham studied harmony and began composing music while Dale and his sisters were young. A few of the compositions were published. "Dad

(Left) W. H. Oldham (with family, 1898)   (Right) In the late 1930s

had also studied sight reading and used to go about singing our gospel songs by note," Dale wrote.[3] The whole family liked to sing, with Dale's sister, Faith, playing the parlor organ.

Oldham retired to a farm he purchased not far from Rushville, Indiana. He and his wife lived there until physical disabilities forced a move to an apartment. W. H. Oldham died November 19, 1945, at the age of seventy.

Draw Me Close to Thee

"I have set the Lord always before me. Because he is at my right hand, I will not be shaken."—Psalm 16:8

Clara M. Brooks

C.M.wR.
DRAW ME CLOSE
W. H. Oldham

1 I would be near-er, my Sav - ior, Where I can hear Thy voice
2 I would be kept in Thy pres - ence, Free from the strife of tongues;
3 Keep me, O Lord, in Thy shad - ow, When the dark tem - pests low'r;
4 Swift-ly the shad-ows are deep-'ning, Light of my life, be near;

1 Fall - ing in ten - der - est whis - pers, Mak - ing my heart re - joice.
2 There shall the hum-ble a - dore Thee, Rais-ing their grate - ful songs.
3 Safe - ly to rest on Thy bos - om, Keep me for - ev - er - more.
4 Strength-en the trust I am keep - ing, Fill me with hope and cheer.

Draw me close to Thee, Draw me close to Thee;
Sav - ior, draw me close to Thee, Sav - ior, draw me close to Thee;

Keep me, dear Sav-ior, so near Thy side, Draw me close to Thee. A - men.

67

Draw Me Close to Thee

In 1911, when the hymn "Draw Me Close to Thee" was published in the songbook *Select Hymns*, the music composer, W. H. Oldham, was pastoring in Clinton, Iowa. The poem writer Clara Brooks and husband, Hiram, were living and pastoring in Denver, Colorado.

No indication seems to be given about how the collaboration on the hymn took place, but Clara Brooks is listed as one of the four editor/compilers of the hymnbook. Perhaps Oldham had written his composition earlier (one songbook lists 1909) and had sent it to the Gospel Trumpet Company. Brooks may have added words to the composition during the editing and compiling process in Anderson.

"Draw Me Close to Thee" was one of a small number of new compositions used in *Select Hymns*. The hymnbook was largely a collection of songs and hymns from earlier songbooks.

The editors' reasoning behind the production of *Select Hymns* can be seen in these words taken from the preface: "It is hoped that the bringing together of this great number of hymns, many of which have been unused for years, will make more effective that part of the reformation work that is carried by song, and will also advance the praise of Him unto whom alone all praise belongs."

11

Clara M. Brooks:

With a Burden for the Lost

In 1903, John G. Neff and his wife, who were serving in a new mission in Delta, Colorado, invited a nineteen-year-old evangelist from Grand Junction, fifty miles away, to come and help them in their ministry. They had met the young woman earlier in Kansas when her family was living there. She accepted their invitation. Her name was Clara McAlister.

A few years later, in 1907, Clara McAlister joined the Trumpet Family in Anderson, Indiana, working for the Gospel Trumpet Company between evangelistic meetings.

Clara was a poet and her gift helped produce a songbook for the Church of God called *Truth in Song.* Besides penning the words of some thirty-five new songs appearing in that volume, she worked in the editing and compiling process.

In the introduction to *Truth in Song* is found this tribute: "We are thankful for the advantage had with this book, of the competent assistance of Sister Clara McAlister and Brother C. W. Naylor, whose earnest and patient efforts in the way of criticism and revision have brought the words of these hymns to a degree of superior excellence."

Clara wrote other poetry not made into song. In fact, fourteen of her poems were included in a compilation called *Treasures of Poetry*, which the Gospel Trumpet Company published in 1913. Her poems also appeared from time to time in the *Gospel Trumpet.*

In June 1909 Clara McAlister married Hiram A. Brooks, a minister from Canada. They served in several locations

Clara M. Brooks

around the country as well as in Canada—sometimes with Hiram as pastor and Clara as assistant pastor; sometimes with Clara as pastor and Hiram as evangelist in the area.

One break in their pastoral ministry came in 1919 and 1920 when Clara, with four children in tow, found herself back in Anderson, while Hiram served a short-term missionary assignment in Europe. She wrote on missionary topics for the *Gospel Trumpet.* She also reported on the missionary conferences at the 1919 and 1920 Anderson Camp Meetings.

Clara Brooks must have had a heart for missions. In one article she wrote, "Yes, missions are ours! They are ours for a lifetime period of service. Ours to cherish, to nourish; the lost millions are ours to bear upward till they reach their home."[1]

Little has been written about Clara McAlister Brooks, but from the words she wrote in prose, poem, and song, we can catch a glimpse of her spirit: her burden for lost souls, her love of beauty, her wonder at the majesty of God, and her fervor for following her Lord.

All the Way

All the way through life's dark journey
Wandered I alone and sad;
Filled with pride and fond ambition,
Naught of joy or peace I had.
Then there came a gentle whisper,
"Wanderer, no longer stray.
I will satisfy your longings
If you'll follow all the way.

"All the way," my lips repeated,
While I turned me quickly round,
Saw my Savior's blood-stained footprints
he had left upon the ground,
Saw his visage marred by sorrow,
Saw the thorns he wore one day,
Saw the way from earth to glory—
"Lord, I'll follow all the way."

—"All the Way" by Clara M. Brooks, from *Treasures of Poetry* (Anderson, IN: Gospel Trumpet Company, 1913), 501.

What a Mighty God We Serve!

Early in 1907 a new songbook was being compiled. Many new songs were being added. A group of songwriters met to iron out the details and put together new songs for the book. They met in the music room owned by the Gospel Trumpet Company. Among those diligently working on the songs were A. L. Byers, C. E. Hunter, Clara McAlister (later, Brooks), C. W. Naylor, D. O. Teasley, and Barney Warren.

One day Barney Warren was visualizing the wonders and beauties of God's world—the Rocky Mountains, the Grand Canyon, waterfalls, flowing rivers, open plains, mighty oceans, and starry heavens. He had a melody of song in mind.

Warren shared this mind picture with Clara McAlister and sang his melody to her. She caught the vision immediately and said, "The music in that chorus seems to say, 'What a mighty God we serve!' "

In a short time the song was finished and on its way into the new songbook *Truth in Song.*

In writing of the incident later, Warren said of Clara McAlister, "Her inspiration for writing the words of this hymn seemed to be at the peak."[2]

"What a Mighty God We Serve!" is a song that is still being sung today.

What A Mighty God We Serve!

" . . . the Lord is the everlasting God, the Creator of the ends of the earth."
—Isaiah 40:28b

Clara M. Brooks

8.7.8.7.wR.
MIGHTY GOD
Barney E. Warren

1 Our Fa-ther's won-drous works we see In the earth and sea and sky;
2 The rag-ing winds and waves are calm, When He says to them, "Be still";
3 He mak-eth worlds by His com-mand, Weighs the moun-tains great and high;
4 Our God, to save from sin's con-trol, Gave His Son a sac-ri-fice;
Por su po-der Dios pu-do criar El gran cie-lo tie-rray mar;

1 He rules o'er all in maj-es-ty, From His roy-al throne on high.
2 The heav-ens praise Him in a psalm, And the an-gels do His will.
3 Cre-ates the wa-ters in His hand, Spans the loft-y, star-lit sky.
4 His grace, a-bound-ing in the soul, Makes the earth a par-a-dise.
Sos-tie-ne al mun-do con bon-dad Y su-pre-ma ma-jes-tad.

What a might-y God we serve! What a might-y God we serve!
we serve! we serve!
¡Oh, qué grande es nues-tro Dios! ¡Oh, qué grande es nues-tro Dios!

Reign-ing now a-bove on His throne of love, What a might-y God we serve!
Rei-na en ma-jes-tad, Rei-na con bon-dad; ¡Oh, qué grande es nues-tro Dios!

73

Lucena and E. E. Byrum

12

Lucena C. Byrum: Poet and Evangelist

Lucena Caroline Beardslee was born in 1882. From Seattle, Washington, she came to work for the Gospel Trumpet Company in 1904. The company was then located in Moundsville, West Virginia, and E. E. Byrum was editor in chief.

She moved with the company to Anderson in 1906. In 1907 she began editing a new Sunday school paper called *Our Little Folks*, published for very young children. It joined *The Shining Light*, which was already being published for older children.

Lucena Beardslee wrote poetry, and on occasion a poem would appear in the children's paper she edited. Other poems found their way into the pages of the *Gospel Trumpet*. Two poems were preserved in Church of God songbooks: "In His Love Let Me Hide" and "A Living Sacrifice."

The year 1908 proved to be a year of significant change for Lucena, and that change involved the E. E. Byrum family. In September 1907, Enoch Byrum's wife, Rhoda, had died after being stricken with typhoid fever. Six children were left without a mother—the oldest child was seventeen years old, while the youngest was five months.

In October 1908 Enoch Byrum and Lucena Beardslee were married, and as Enoch wrote later, Lucena "assumed the responsibilities of the home as a wife and caretaker of my motherless children."[1] It must have been quite an undertaking; though three of the children were teen-agers, the other three were ten, nearly eight, and one-and-a-half years in age.

In His Love Let Me Hide

"Therefore, since we have been justified through faith, we have peace with God through our Lord Jesus Christ."—Romans 5:1

Lucena C. Byrum

LET ME HIDE
Andrew L. Byers

1 Let me walk in the path which my Sav - ior has trod, Let me
2 Let my heart e'er be fixed on my trea - sures a - bove, Let the
3 Do you ask why I love Him the dear - est of all? Why so
4 It is bless - ed to serve Him and do His good will, For so

1 fol - low so close by His side; For by trust - ing in Him I am
2 plea-sures of earth fade a - way; For there's noth - ing so love - ly as
3 free - ly I yield un - to Him? 'Tis be - cause He has loved me and
4 pre - cious to me is His love; Let my tal - ents and time all be

1 hap - py and free, In the fold of His love let me hide.
2 Je - sus to me, Let me ne'er from His love go a - stray.
3 died on the cross, My poor soul lost in sin to re - deem.
4 giv - en to Him, Till He calls me to meet Him a - bove.

In His love let me hide, In His
In the fold of His love let me hide,

love let me hide (let me hide); For by trust-ing in Him I am
In the fold of His love let me hide;

hap - py and free, In the fold of His love let me hide (let me hide).

She must have been equal to the task, however, for her husband paid her this tribute: "Her true devotion to the family and contentment and love of married life, with her deep spirituality, [have] enabled us to have a congenial Christian home."[2]

Lucena entered the ministry in 1919, and was listed in the yearbook as an evangelist. Ordained in 1923, she accompanied her husband in evangelistic work in the United States, Canada, and even on two tours to the West Indies, South America, and Central America.

Outliving Enoch by fourteen years, Lucena Byrum died February 21, 1956, at seventy-four years of age.

In His Love Let Me Hide

"In His Love Let Me Hide" appeared for the first time in 1907 in *Truth in Song*, but under a different title: "My Heart's Desire." The words were written by Lucena C. Beardslee and the tune set by A. L. Byers.

We don't know the setting in which this song was composed. The editors of *Truth in Song* wrote in a preface to the songbook, "It has been our aim . . . to represent as many contributors as possible. Many excellent compositions, some of words and some of music, have been furnished by others." They were also looking primarily to use first-time songs.

Lucena Beardslee was a Gospel Trumpet worker whose poems were printed from time to time in the *Trumpet*. It is probable that the songbook editors had access to this already-existing poem of hers and judged it as worthy of inclusion in the songbook; and so Byers set to work to compose music for it.

The song stresses an abiding relationship with Christ, and in its first printing was listed under the topic "Abiding." By the time it appeared in *Hymns and Spiritual Songs* at the end of the 1920s, the song's name had changed to the present one, and Lucena C. Beardslee had become Lucena C. Byrum.

Meditation

Softly now the sunlight's fading,
Evening breezes gently blow,
Shadows 'round me fast are gath'ring,
For the evening sun is low.

Comes a thought of meditation,
Scanning now the day just past;
What have I for God accomplished,
Were this day to be my last?

Were my actions kind and tender
To my friends and loved ones dear?
Have I heartache caused another?
Have I caused a sigh or tear?

Silently I sit and ponder,
I the day in thought retrace:
Were there any deeds of kindness
have I filled a Christian's place?

Now my tho'ts are turning heavenward,
To the God who rules the day.
May I scatter deeds of kindness
All along my pilgrim way.

—from poem "Meditation,"by Lucena C. Beardslee, *Gospel Trumpet* (October 24, 1907), 2.

13

Mildred E. Howard:

Continuing the Heritage

When Mildred E. Howard was born in 1884, she came into a pioneer Church of God family. Just four years earlier, her father, J. N. Howard, had heard A. J. Kilpatrick preach a sermon on sanctification, had sought the experience, and renewed his call to the ministry. He began preaching in the vicinity of Payne, Ohio. Mildred's uncle, George W. Howard, joined her father in the ministry in 1885.

Mildred E. Howard

These were the days of the "flying ministry." Ministers held evangelistic meetings for several weeks and went on to another place and another meeting. Later editor F. G. Smith wrote of those early preaching days of J. N. Howard: "In the early days of the work Brother and Sister Howard traveled extensively with team and wagon, preaching the truth and raising up congregations. A number of preachers were saved under his preaching."[1]

Into this kind of setting, Mildred was born, as well as other siblings. We do not have a record of the particulars of her early life, but we do know she herself had entered the ministry by 1912, and possibly earlier than that. Even before that, she had been traveling with her father, helping in evangelistic meetings in Kentucky, Indiana, Ohio, and Michigan.

In a 1907 field report, Mildred and her father had this to say, "We had one service at Winchester, Ky., and came on to Anderson. We expect to go from here to Ft. Wayne, Ind., and stay over Sunday; then home. Truly the harvest is plenteous and the laborers few. Souls are daily perishing, so let us all do with all our might what our hands find to do, and the Lord will richly reward us. Yours in his service, all for God and his cause, and souls who are perishing, J. N. Howard. Mildred E. Howard."[2]

She wrote the words to one song that has survived through the years and is still sung by Church of God congregations—"Consecration"—but we have no record of an extensive writing career. Her father's name, however, appears frequently in the *Trumpet* in the early years. Perhaps she was content to remain in the background, serving behind the scenes.

Father and daughter teamed up as pastor and assistant pastor in 1921, probably a year after Mildred was ordained. For ten years they served pastorates in Nappanee, Claypool, and Indianapolis, Indiana. The partnership ended when J. N. Howard died in 1931.

Mildred Howard served for a time as instructor at Winchester Academy, a Church of God-sponsored school for grades 1-12 in Winchester, Kentucky. She also worked with the Women's Missionary Society (now Women of the Church of God) at the national level as an officer. She was parliamentarian for that organization from its beginning in the early thirties until 1959. She died in Indianapolis in 1967 in her early eighties.

Time Speeds Away

> Time speeds away, away, away,
> Another hour, another day,
> Another month, another year,
> The end of time will soon be here.

An awful, yet a glorious day!
Oh, joy to all who've left sin's way!
But awful doom for all in sin,
"Depart, ye cannot enter in."

Thus time will end—the end must come,
And with the end great grief to some.
His saints shall meet him in the air,
Forever dwell in heaven fair.

—From "Time Speeds Away,"by Mildred Howard,
Gospel Trumpet (March 21, 1907), 2.

Consecration

The words and music to "Consecration" were likely written shortly before its inclusion in *Truth in Song* in 1907. A. L. Byers, one of the editors of that songbook, set the music for Mildred Howard's song poem.

The song first appeared with five verses plus the chorus. With the song's inclusion in the 1971 *Hymnal of the Church of God*, the third verse was dropped. Verse three carried a foreign missions emphasis: "Tho' he may call across the sea,/ With Jesus I will go,/ And tell the lost of love so free/ Till all his pow'r may know."

Another change that came about over the years is in one phrase in the chorus. By 1926 (*Melodies of Zion*), the phrase "I'll serve thee, Lord, thine own to be" had been changed to "I'll serve thee, Lord, and faithful be."

The title "Consecration" sets forth the topic that the rest of the song tries to define and explain. It is a prayer, a commitment to total submission to God and the service of God.

One year before her song appeared, Mildred Howard had written an article in the *Gospel Trumpet* about this subject. She wrote, "When I came to [God], worldly aspirations and ambitions, visions of honor and fame, and desire for the applause of this world, were all forsaken, and now my greatest ambition is to be just what He wants me to be and meet his highest expectation of me."³

"Consecration" was the poet's prayer.

Consecration

" . . . Now, who is willing to consecrate himself today to the Lord?"
—I Chronicles 29:5b

Mildred E. Howard

C.M.wR.
CONSECRATION
Andrew L. Byers

1 Since Je - sus gave His life for me Should I not give Him mine?
2 I care not where my Lord di-rects, His pur-pose I'll ful - fill;
3 My home and friends are dear to me, Yet He is dear - er still;
4 My all, O Lord, to Thee I give, Ac - cept it as Thine own;

1 I'm con - se-crat - ed, Lord, to Thee, I shall be whol - ly Thine.
2 I know He ev - 'ry one pro-tects Who does His ho - ly will.
3 In my af-fec - tion first He'll be, And first His right - eous will.
4 For Thee a-lone I'll ev - er live, My heart shall be Thy throne.

My life, O Lord, I give to Thee, My tal - ents, time and all; I'll

serve Thee, Lord, and faith-ful be, I'll hear Thy faint-est call. A - men.

14

Lawrence E. Brooks:
Keeping Close Touch

"I was born in January of 1894. My first contact with this movement was during the year 1905. I was converted in 1915, started my ministry that same year, and attended my first Anderson Camp Meeting in 1917. I have been in close touch with the history of this reform movement from then until now."[1]

So wrote Lawrence E. Brooks some sixty years later as a brief summary of himself—and he did stay close to the movement's workings and history.

He spent more than twenty years in pastoring churches, serving congregations in Hot Springs and Little Rock, Arkansas; Hickman and Louisville, Kentucky; Terre Haute and Anderson, Indiana; St. Paul, Minnesota; Cleveland, Ohio; and St. Louis, Missouri. While in Anderson he attended Anderson Bible Training School.

In 1920 Lawrence Brooks married Vena Miller, and over the next few years two children were born to them.

Lawrence Brooks's name was seen occasionally in the *Gospel Trumpet.* In 1921 he wrote about an answer to prayer and concluded with: "My soul is made to magnify God for his goodness to me, as I review my life since I started in his service and call to mind the many times he has in a miraculous way supplied my needs and helped me, right in the face of severe financial and other difficulties, to stay in his service. How it increases my faith and encourages me to be eternally true to God and my calling!"[2]

Brooks also wrote poetry. A handful of his poems were

Lawrence E. Brooks

set to music and appeared in *His Praise Anew* in 1936. One of these "He Lifted Me Out" survived through successive hymnals to today.

Besides pastoring and writing, Brooks served the church in other ways. He became a promoter of the new graded Sunday school curriculum for the Gospel Trumpet Company in 1937. He spent the year traveling to congregations in various states "helping schools with their problems and promoting the new Christian Life Sunday-school literature."[3]

Brooks also stayed in close touch with the movement in

the administration of the wider Church of God work. He was a field representative for World Service from 1945 to 1947. In 1947 he had the added responsibility of registrar of the Clergy Bureau (which later became the Division of Church Service) and for eight years headed up the work of getting the church yearbook out. He served as secretary of the General Ministerial Assembly for eight years.

Over the years the General Ministerial Assembly had discussed the need for a pension plan for ministers. In 1948 the assembly set a plan for a Pension Board into motion with Brooks as the first executive secretary-treasurer. The plan went into operation in 1949, and Brooks guided that operation for the next eleven years.

Lawrence E. Brooks died August 2, 1979, at the age of eighty-five, after sixty-four years of keeping close to God's work in the church. Shortly before his death, in an evaluation of the Church of God movement, Brooks wrote: "It is great to know that God has brought us through this first 100 years. We have not grown rapidly in numbers, but in many other respects we have made great strides. I honestly believe that God now can depend upon this movement to do his work in a way that he has not been able to do before. I have faith for the future."[4]

He Lifted Me Out

The song "He Lifted Me Out" was first printed in *His Praise Anew* in 1936. In his memoirs written in 1974, Lawrence E. Brooks told how the song came into being:

> One of my best years in Cleveland was 1934. In the month of May that year, K. Y. Plank conducted a two-weeks revival. I was greatly concerned for the revival effort, and I made it a habit during the meeting to get up an hour before the family and spend this time in meditation and prayer.
>
> One morning while [I was] in a mood of thanksgiv-

He Lifted Me Out

"He lifted me out of the slimy pit, out of the mud and mire."—Psalm 40:2b

Lawrence E. Brooks
Harm. by K. Y. Plank

HE LIFTED ME OUT
Lawrence E. Brooks

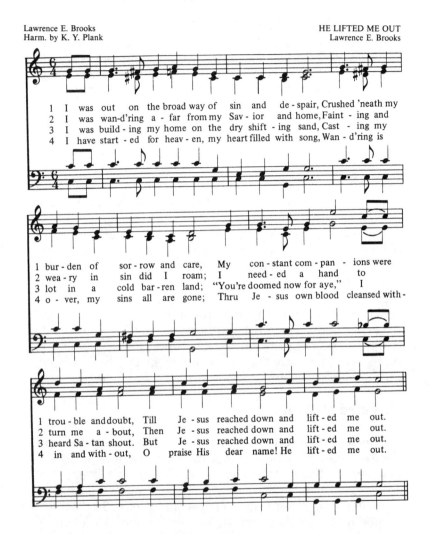

1. I was out on the broad way of sin and de-spair, Crushed 'neath my
2. I was wan-d'ring a-far from my Sav-ior and home, Faint-ing and
3. I was build-ing my home on the dry shift-ing sand, Cast-ing my
4. I have start-ed for heav-en, my heart filled with song, Wan-d'ring is

1. bur-den of sor-row and care, My con-stant com-pan-ions were
2. wea-ry in sin did I roam; I need-ed a hand to
3. lot in a cold bar-ren land; "You're doomed now for aye," I
4. o-ver, my sins all are gone; Thru Je-sus own blood cleansed with-

1. trou-ble and doubt, Till Je-sus reached down and lift-ed me out.
2. turn me a-bout, Then Je-sus reached down and lift-ed me out.
3. heard Sa-tan shout. But Je-sus reached down and lift-ed me out.
4. in and with-out, O praise His dear name! He lift-ed me out.

He lift-ed me out of the deep mir - y clay; He set-tled my feet
in the strait, nar-row way; He lift-ed me up to a heav-en-ly place,
And flood-eth my soul each day with His grace.

ing, a poem began to take shape in my mind. I secured paper and pencil and within about twenty minutes I had written the song "He Lifted Me Out." As I wrote the song, the melody came very clear. An hour later when Rev. Plank came down to breakfast, he went to the piano. I hummed the melody over and he picked it up on the piano. In a short time we were singing the song.

I managed to make a couple of hand copies of the music and in the month of August at our state camp meeting at Springfield, Ohio, . . . Marie Gorsuch and I sang the song as a soprano and alto duet in one morning service. Before we were finished, some of the people were shouting and coming to the altar. The preacher had no chance to bring his message, for the service and the altar service lasted for an hour and a half.

Share with Others

If life you spend for self alone,
And all you make you call your own,
And pile it up within your store,
While reaching out to gather more,
You think that you'll be happy then,
When all your goods are gathered in.
But then, alas! you will awake,
Discover then your sad mistake:
You failed to share with others.

True happiness cannot be found
Where coveteousness and pride abound.
To covet means to close your heart
And bid all else but self depart;
Then as you struggle for your goal,
Hell takes a mortgage on your soul.
"This night thy soul's required of thee;
Then whose will all of these things be!"
That you have kept from others?

O selfish soul, you'll never reach
The goal in life for which you seek.
It's like the legend heard of old,
Of how to find a pot of gold:
Just when you think you've found the spot,
You then awake to find you've not.
You've missed your road; you need to turn
And a very precious lesson learn—
That you must share with others.

—"Share with Others," by Lawrence Brooks, *Gospel Trumpet* (January 2, 1919), 1.

15

Henry C. Clausen:
First a Christian, then a Musician

"We are coming to realize more and more the value of singing in connection with gospel work," wrote Henry C. Clausen in 1921, "and that it is a special means that God has ordained by which people might express their praise and gratitude to him."[1]

Born in Germany on April 7, 1880, Clausen came to the United States when he was three years old and grew up in Nebraska. He attended a business college and went to work as manager of a lumber company. Though we don't know what part music played in his early life, we know it became important to him later.

He graduated from Moody Bible Institute in Chicago with a diploma in music. He also studied music at Indiana College of Musical Fine Arts in Indianapolis, earning a bachelor of music in 1929, and at Cincinnati Conservatory in Cincinnati, Ohio.

Clausen was preaching and pastoring in North Dakota in 1917, at the same time J. T. Wilson was trying to get the Anderson Bible Training School off the ground. Wilson wrote to Clausen, asking him to come teach music.

"When the brethren first wrote to me about coming to the school," said Clausen, remembering those days, "I wrote them that God had sent me to North Dakota and he would have to move me. A short time after this in the night God made it very plain to me that I should preach my farewell sermons (as we had several appointments) and go to Anderson."[2]

Clausen became one of the first two full-time teachers at

Henry C. Clausen

the school that was later named Anderson College. He taught vocal music and theory for twenty-eight years. During those years he also led the Glad Tidings Chorus, a choir of singers that limited themselves to singing religious music.

The chorus was known for a high spiritual attitude, which undoubtedly was in great part due to the director himself. In 1922 the school management said, "Brother Clausen is a great spiritual asset to the school. He is first a Christian, then a musician."[3]

Besides teaching music, Clausen also did evangelistic work. He sang and led music in camp meetings and other gatherings, including the yearly Anderson camp meeting. For a number of years, this meant conducting that great gathering without the help of a public address system.

Also a composer, Clausen was instrumental in setting to music a number of songs used in Church of God songbooks over the years, many of which were part of the 1918 *Songs of Grace and Glory* songbook. He served as one of the editors of that book.

After retirement from Anderson College in 1945, Clausen traveled for five years in evangelistic work. He then served pastorates in Oakland City, Indiana, and Albion, Nebraska. In 1957 he suffered a stroke. He died in 1960.

Music was important to Clausen, and he helped impress students and others with its importance. But something else was more important. As he said upon his retirement, "While one can always look back and see where he might have done better, yet during this time I have never turned my back on my Savior. . . . I would not take worlds for the freedom I have in God. I am tied to nothing but him."[4]

He Wants His Way in Thee

The year was 1918. Three men—A. L. Byers, D. O. Teasley, and H. C. Clausen—met in Anderson to put together a new medium-size songbook. Some of the old standard church hymns were included, but many new songs, never in print before, were added.

H. C. Clausen, a composer of tunes, teamed up with several song poem writers to form some new songs. One song poem writer was Charles Naylor, a heavy contributor to our store of heritage songs. Of the five songs Naylor and Clausen wrote for *Songs of Grace and Glory*, one is still in our hymnal today: "He Wants His Way in Thee."

He Wants His Way in Thee

*" . . . And this is how we know that He lives in us: We know it by the Spirit he
gave us."—I John 3:24b,c*

Charles W. Naylor

HIS WAY IN THEE
Henry C. Clausen

1 God has sent the Ho - ly Spir - it To our hearts an hon-ored guest,
2 Let the Spir - it do the plan - ning, Point the way thy feet shall go;
3 He doth some-times work in si - lence, When thou dost not know at all;
4 All thy - self to Him sur-ren - der, As He pleas - es let Him do;

1 To de - liv - er us from e - vil, And to bring us peace and rest.
2 Great-er than thine own His wis-dom, He the will of God doth know;
3 He doth some-times speak so soft-ly Thou must lis - ten for His call.
4 In the paths He lead-eth, fol-low, Wheth-er they be old or new.

1 He has come to work with-in us Heav-en's pur - pos - es so blest:
2 Bet - ter, wis - er than thy choos-ing Is the way that He will show:
3 But if thou wilt trust Him ful - ly, He will be thine all in all:
4 When the tasks seem hard be - fore thee, He with pow - er will en - due:

1 He wants His way in thee. Yield un - to the Ho - ly
2 He wants His way in thee.
3 He wants His way in thee.
4 He wants His way in thee.

Spir - it, Let Him have His way with thee;

Be thou read - y to o - bey Him, He leads to vic - to - ry.

The specific circumstances of the writing of this song are not known. The general circumstance—the need for new songs for the songbook—likely spurred the authors to write. Possibly no special story accompanied the birth of the song.

Of the writing of his song poems in general, Naylor had this to say.

> Most of the songs that I have written have nothing of interest connected with their origin. Often just the subject comes into the mind and with it a sort of inspiration to write. Sometimes a bit of melody gets to running through my mind and almost unconsciously words begin to fit themselves to it. . . . Sometimes I see the need for a song on a certain line and just deliberately set to work and write it, without any particular inspiration. I simply do it like I do anything else.
>
> Quite frequently I am not able to express in words the depths and fullness that I see and feel in the subject. Part of my songs are written with no particular emotion. At other times there are such deep emotions that the very depths of the soul seem stirred, and the heart is poured out into the song till it seems to be a part of myself.[5]

K. Y. Plank as a young man

K. Y. Plank in later years

16

Kinney Y. Plank:

Commitment to Serve

Kinney Y. Plank was born to S. S. and Anna Plank in West Liberty, Ohio, in 1897. By 1910 his father had entered the ministry with the Church of God. Fifteen years later, K. Y. also entered the ministry.

Plank and his wife, Pearl, committed themselves to serving the local church. They worked as a team, he as pastor and she often as leader in Christian education and youth.

Ministry began in Birmingham, Alabama, with K. Y. serving as assistant pastor. He then went on to serve pastorates in Anniston, Alabama; Columbus, Ohio; East Rainelle and Charleston, West Virginia; and Springfield and Ashland, Illinois. Plank also was active in evangelistic work throughout the years before his retirement in 1967.

Plank seemed to carry a burden for lost souls. In a report printed in the *Gospel Trumpet* about the altar room work at the 1949 Anderson Camp Meeting, he wrote, "There is no work that draws one closer to God than that of helping a sinner to know God. There is no more inspiring experience than seeing a penitent soul find release from sin and find new life in Jesus Christ."[1]

He urged Christians to serve Christ through serving others. "It is easy for people," he wrote in a 1945 *Gospel Trumpet* article, "to become so busy in being religious that they forget to be Christian; they fail to be Christian in their attitudes, in love, in mercy, and in humanitarian service. . . . It is easy to talk about following Christ, but if we fail to imitate him in sympathy and compassion we have missed the mark entirely. The devout follower of Christ is one who enters by sympathy and love into the sorrows and joys of others."[2]

By the time Plank was in his late twenties, his interest in music had begun to display itself. He traveled to New York City to study harmony. Not much of a singer, he put his knowledge to work in composition.

Besides writing the words and music to "Prayer of My Heart," he collaborated with Lawrence Brooks on the tune composition of two or three songs for *His Praise Anew*. A new song for which he had written words or music would now and then appear in an issue of the *Gospel Trumpet*. Another song, "Come, Holy Spirit," joined "Prayer of My Heart" in the 1971 *Hymnal of the Church of God*.

In 1952, when a new major Church of God hymnal was in the planning stages, a general committee made up of ministers and music leaders was formed. K. Y. Plank was one of the thirteen members of this committee that set basic policies for the new hymnal and advised the editors. That same year Plank participated in the 1952 Anderson Camp Meeting music committee. The group planned music leaders and specials for the general services, planned daily music conferences, and sponsored the camp meeting choir.

Plank died in November 1975 at the age of seventy-eight. Several years before his death, he wrote, "Come, O Holy Spirit,/ Pour thy love in my soul;/ Teach me how I may serve thee,/ Come, take full control."[3] These words seem to have captured the focus of K. Y. Plank's life: to serve God.

Prayer of My Heart

The time was 1936. Six years had passed since the Gospel Trumpet Company had put out a major songbook, but nearly ten since there had been a major collection of new material.

In *His Praise Anew*, eighty percent of the songs were new. The publishers explained in the forward: "Many new manuscripts have accumulated for the reason that the inspiration for sacred-song composition is not only divine but is more or less constantly manifest in new productions.

"Many old songs have won a permanent place in the repertory of the Christian church, but the new songs, even though some should prove transient, provide a refreshing which gives them a place of usefulness, also."

One of those new songs that was to prove of a lasting rather than transient quality was "Prayer of My Heart," written by K. Y. Plank.

The song was written while Plank was in New York attending the Juilliard School of Music, before his marriage. This seems to have been a time of discouragement and loneliness for him, but also a time of growth. Out of and in spite of his struggles, his prayer was for "A faith unmoved in time of trial,/ That's anchored in my Lord!"

Prayer of My Heart

"But grow in the grace and knowledge of our Lord and Savior Jesus Christ. To him be glory both now and forever! Amen."—II Peter 3:18

C.M.

K. Y. Plank

PRAYER OF MY HEART
K. Y. Plank

1 O for a clos-er walk with God, A life that bears no stain
2 O for a deep-er, rich-er life With treas-ures stored a - bove;
3 O for a faith that's root-ed deep In God's e-ter-nal word;

1 Of earth-ly pride or van-i-ties, A life that's not in vain!
2 A life that soars o'er car-nal strife And nes-tles in God's love!
3 A faith un-moved in time of trial, That's an-chored in my Lord!

Dale Oldham at the microphone

17

W. Dale Oldham:
Leaving His Mark

W. Dale Oldham was born on March 30, 1903, in Oklahoma to Church of God minister William H. Oldham and his wife, Myrtle. At a young age music had a strong hold on his life.

"Music was always important to me," Oldham wrote in his autobiography. "Dad had . . . studied sight reading and used to go about singing our gospel songs by note. I can still hear his 'sol, sol, la, sol, me, do, do, la,' as he had in mind, 'What a Friend We Have in Jesus.' So it was easy for me to pick up the do re mi at an early age, just by listening to him. Long before I could read a book I could sing any tune I knew by note."[1]

Oldham's father had composed music, some of which was published, and later Oldham himself tried his hand at composing. Eleven songs in the 1936 *His Praise Anew* song-book listed W. Dale Oldham as composer of the music. For a few of these, he wrote the words also. One such case was "Let Me See Jesus Only."

After he became a Christian in June 1919, Oldham attended Anderson Bible Training School in Anderson. He was sixteen, with only two years of high school completed, but he managed to finish the two-year course. He became an evangelistic singer, traveling with some of the leading ministers of the day as they held meetings here and there.

In 1922 Oldham felt called to the preaching ministry. He took his first pastorate in Cynthiana, Kentucky, in 1925. By this time he had been married to Pauline E. Brown (Polly) for scarcely a year. The couple moved to other pastorates in Akron and Rochester, Indiana; and Lima and Dayton, Ohio. After eleven years in Dayton, they received the call to pastor Park Place Church in Anderson, Indiana. Oldham remained in the role of pastor there from 1945 until 1962. A new opportunity opened up for Oldham in 1946. That year a student at Anderson College, Richard Meischke, was a part of Oldham's congregation. He was working part time at a local radio station and had a good voice for broadcasting. Oldham remembered, "One day in my office Dick asked with a smile, 'Pastor, do you think it will ever be possible for us to produce a national radio program?'"[2]

From the ensuing conversation, the idea was born for a national radio program by the Church of God. In January of 1947, the first program of "The Christian Brotherhood Hour" was broadcast. The initial recording sessions were held in Park Place Church, with Meischke as announcer, Oldham as speaker, and singing groups from the congregation and college. Oldham held the position of speaker until 1968.

Oldham was a published author as well as a speaker and a singer. Some of his better known books are *Giants Along My Path, Just Across the Street* (later reprinted under the title *How to Grow Spiritually*), and *Living Close to God.*

Active in the national life of the Church of God, Oldham served on the Warner Press Publication Board and Anderson College Board of Trustees for a number of years. He also served several years as vice-chair of the General Assembly.

W. Dale Oldham died in 1984 after a battle with cancer. He was 81. He had made significant contribution to God's kingdom and the Church of God movement. As was said of him in a memorial issue of *Vital Christianity*: "Dale Oldham, through his faithfulness to his calling, has put his mark on this movement—an achievement few will ever duplicate."[3]

Where Crossroads Meet

There is a place where crossroads meet,
And every man should know
Decision time has come for him—
Which way, now, will he go?

The left road downward takes its course,
Small effort needed there;
But to the right the path ascends,
And one is called to dare.

Pause thoughtfully where crossroads meet,
Consider well your choice;
Inquire of God, bid truth to speak,
Give heed then to his voice.

Eternity is here involved,
More than a road you choose;
Your destiny, eternal life?
If not, your all you lose.

Consider well e'er you decide
To left or right you'll go;
Omniscient God leads but one way—
The high way, not the low.

The road is steep; It calls for strength,
And much may yet befall;
But climb with God, in joy or pain,
The summit's worth it all.

—"Where Crossroads Meet" by W. Dale Oldham, written in 1979, printed in *Vital Christianity* (December 1989), 43.

Let Me See Jesus Only

"When they looked up, they saw no one except Jesus."—Matthew 17:8

W. Dale Oldham

JESUS ONLY
W. Dale Oldham

1 Dead to ev - 'ry world-ly pleas-ure, Dead in - deed to sin am I;
2 Let me strive not for the rich - es Of this earth that soon de - cay;
3 Storms in fu - ry beat a - round me, Tem-pests oft my heart as - sail;
4 When I face death's chill-y riv - er, When up - on its brink I stand,

1 But a - live to Christ my Sav-ior, Dai-ly to Him I'm draw-ing nigh.
2 From the world I've turned to Je - sus And His more a - bun - dant way.
3 But my Pi - lot's name is Je - sus, He will calm the wild - est gale.
4 I shall fear - less be if Je - sus Leads me gen - tly by the hand.

1-3 Let me see
Let me see Je-sus on - ly, Je-sus on - ly, Je-sus on-ly;
4 Then I'll see
Then I'll see

Let me see
Let me see Je-sus on - ly, On-ly He can sat - is - fy.
Then I'll see
Then I'll see

104

Let Me See Jesus Only

"Strangely enough, this song was written in the home of my mother-in-law," said W. Dale Oldham one time in talking about the song "Let Me See Jesus Only."

The year was 1936 and Dale Oldham and his wife, Polly, had been visiting Polly's mother in Huntington, Indiana. Polly and her mother were out shopping. Dale was alone in the house. Two Scripture verses came to his mind: John 12:21, which says, "Sir, we would see Jesus"; and Matthew 17:8, which says "When they had lifted up their eyes, they saw no man, save Jesus only."

"I put the two scriptures together and came up with the song," said Oldham.

"Let Me See Jesus Only" was first published in the 1936 songbook *His Praise Anew*. It is still sung today and has been sung in other countries and languages.

Dale Oldham leading music

Notes

Introduction

1. A. L. Byers, *Birth of a Reformation* (Anderson, Ind: Gospel Trumpet Company, 1921), 393.

2. Byers 393-4.

3. Byers 394.

4. H. M. Riggle, *Pioneer Evangelism* (Anderson, Ind: Gospel Trumpet Company, 1924), 91.

5. B. E. Warren and D. S. Warner, *Echoes from Glory* (Grand Junction, Mich: Gospel Trumpet Company, 1893), preface.

Chapter 1

1. Byers 40.

2. C. E. Brown, *When the Trumpet Sounded* (Anderson, Ind: Warner Press, 1951), 50.

3. Brown 55.

4. Byers 407.

5. Byers 9.

6. "Song Stories," *Gospel Trumpet* (Jan. 14, 1939).10.

7. "Song Stories," *Gospel Trumpet* (Feb. 11, 1939), 10.

8. "Song Stories," *Gospel Trumpet* (Apr. 1, 1939), 10.

9. "Song Stories," *Gospel Trumpet* (May 20, 1939), 12.

10. *Gospel Trumpet* (Jan. 15, 1891), 2.

Chapter 2

1. Byers 330.

2. Byers 330.

3. Harold L. Phillips, *A Miracle of Survival* (Anderson, Ind: Warner Press, 1979), 34.

4. Byers 411.

5. John W. V. Smith, *Quest for Holiness and Unity* (Anderson, Ind: Warner Press, 1980), 66.

6 Smith 66.

Chapter 3

1. Axchie Bolitho, *To the Chief Singer* (Anderson, Ind: Gospel Trumpet Company, 1942), 20.
2. Bolitho 19.
3. Bolitho 76.
4. Smith 73.
5. *Gospel Trumpet* (May 26, 1951), 16.
6. Smith 74.
7. "Song Stories," *Gospel Trumpet* (Oct. 15, 1938), 10.
8. "Song Stories," *Gospel Trumpet* (Oct. 8, 1938), 10.
9. Bolitho 110.
10. Bolitho 111.
11. "Song Stories," *Gospel Trumpet* (Feb. 18, 1939), 10.
12. "Song Stories," *Gospel Trumpet* (Nov. 19, 1938), 10.
13. "Song Stories," *Gospel Trumpet* (Sept. 17, 1938), 10.
14. Bolitho 128-9.
15. Bolitho 168.
16. Bolitho 169.
17. Bolitho 171.

Chapter 4

1. *Gospel Trumpet* (Jan. 15, 1891), 3.
2. Brown 304.
3. *Gospel Trumpet* (Feb. 3, 1945), 19.
4. Brown 155.
5. "Song Stories," *Gospel Trumpet* (Aug. 13, 1938), 10.

Chapter 5

1. Andrew L. Byers, "Sacred Song," *Gospel Trumpet* (May 6, 1926), 6.
2. Brown 145.
3. Byers 1926, 6.
4. "Song Stories," *Gospel Trumpet* (Aug. 13, 1938), 10.
5. Byers 1926, 7.
6. "Song Stories," *Gospel Trumpet* (July 30, 1938), 10.
7. W Dale Oldham "A. L. Byers," *Gospel Trumpet* (Dec. 13, 1952), 12.

Chapter 6
1. Smith 371-2.
2. *Gospel Trumpet* (Jan. 12, 1893), 2.
3. Smith 185.
4. *Gospel Trumpet* (Dec. 7, 1935), 15.

Chapter 7
1. C. W. Naylor, *When Adversity Comes* (Anderson, Ind: Gospel Trumpet Company, 1944), 8-9.
2. Brown 181.
3. C. W. Naylor, *The Secret of the Singing Heart* (Anderson, Ind: Gospel Trumpet Company, 1930), 127.
4. "How the Songs Were Written," *Gospel Trumpet* (Sept. 7, 1922), 15.
5. "How the Songs Were Written," *Gospel Trumpet* (Sept. 21, 1922), 4.

Chapter 8
1. C. E. Hunter, "Poetry for Hymn Use," *Gospel Trumpet* (Oct. 5, 1899), 4.
2. "How the Songs Were Written," *Gospel Trumpet* (Oct. 19, 1922), 4.
3. *Gospel Trumpet* (Sept. 3, 1903), 4.

Chapter 9
1. Brown 223-224.
2. *Gospel Trumpet* (Jan. 21, 1904), 5.
3. W. Dale Oldham, *Giants Along My Path* (Anderson, Ind: Warner Press, 1973), 107.
4. Phillips 153.
5. Oldham 108
6. "How the Songs Were Written," *Gospel Trumpet* (Nov. 9, 1922), 8.
7. "How the Songs Were Written," *Gospel Trumpet* (Dec. 28, 1922), 12.

Chapter 10
1. Brown 289.
2. *Gospel Trumpet* (Jan. 12, 1946), 20.
3. Oldham 37.

Chapter 11
1. "Our Maternal Responsibility for Missions," *Gospel Trumpet* (Anderson, Ind: Gospel Trumpet Company), Nov. 20, 1919, 13.
2. "Song Stories," *Gospel Trumpet* (Nov. 26, 1938), 10.

Chapter 12
1. E. E. Byrum, *Life Experiences* (Anderson, Ind: Gospel Trumpet Company, 1928), 116.

Chapter 13
1. F. G. Smith, "Another Pioneer Gone Home," *Gospel Trumpet* (Aug. 13, 1931), 20.
2. *Gospel Trumpet* (Feb. 21, 1907), 13.
3. Mildred E. Howard, "The Christian's Recompense" *Gospel Trumpet* (Jan. 25, 1906), 3.

Chapter 14
1. Lawrence E. Brooks, "The Problem of Our Own Narrowness," The First Century, Vol. II (Anderson, Ind: Warner Press, 1979), 107.
2. Lawrence Brooks, "Relieved of a Fifty-dollar Debt in Answer to Prayer," *Gospel Trumpet* (July 14, 1921), 28.
3. A. T. Rowe, "Lawrence E. Brooks in Sunday-school Work," *Gospel Trumpet* (Jan. 23, 1937), 13.
4. Brooks, "The Problem of Our Own Narrowness," in Barry Callen's *The First Century* (Anderson, Ind: Warner Press, 1979), 109.

Chapter 15
1. *Gospel Trumpet* (Jan. 20, 1921), 28.
2. *Gospel Trumpet* (May 19, 1945), 5.
3. *Gospel Trumpet* (Sept. 14, 1922), 15.

4. *Gospel Trumpet* (May 19, 1945), 5.
5. *Gospel Trumpet* (Aug. 24, 1922), 9.

Chapter 16
1. K. Y. Plank, "Altar Services at the Camp Meeting," *Gospel Trumpet* (July 23, 1949), 5.
2. K. Y. Plank, "Ye Have Done It unto Me," *Gospel Trumpet* (Feb. 24, 1945), 5.
3. "Come, Holy Spirit," *Hymnal of the Church of God* (Anderson, Ind: Warner Press, 1971), no. 139.

Chapter 17
1. Oldham 37.
2. Oldham 241.
3. *Vital Christianity* (July 29, 1984), 6.

Alphabetical Index of Authors

Alphabetical Index of Songs

(* — We have no record of these poems being developed into songs.)

DATE DUE